A Journey Toward
Purpose and Promise

Dr. Brandy S. Peoples

ISBN: 978-1-7347748-0-1 (Paperback)

Library of Congress Control Number: 2020905235

Scripture quotations marked (AMP) are taken from the AM-PLIFIED Bible 2015, Copyright © 1954, 1958, 1962, 1964, 1965, 1987 by the Lockman Foundation. Used by permission.

Scripture quotations marked (KJV) are taken from the Holy Bible, KING JAMES VERSION, in public domain.

Scripture quotations marked (NIV) are taken from the Holy Bible, NEW INTERNATIONAL VERSION®, NIV® Copyright © 1973, 1978, 1984, 2011 by Biblica, Inc.® Used by permission of Zondervan. All rights reserved worldwide.

Edited by Shelia E. Bell www.sheliawritesbooks.com
Book Design by MMADHOUSE Media
Photography by Elijah Sharks
Hair & Makeup by Tiffany Perfect

Dr. Brandy S. Peoples
P. O. Box 264
Hazelwood, MO 63042
www.drbrandyspeoples.com

To the Moses in my life, who've led the way but couldn't journey with me...
Mr. B.T., Dorothea, Leon, and Fay.
I love you.

To my parents, Marvin and Robin...
Like Joshua and Caleb, you fearlessly led me to something that was much bigger than what you dreamed.
Thank you.

Joshua 1:3 (KJV), "Every place that the sole of your foot shall tread upon, that have I given unto you...."

Table of Contents

Preface

If I were to be totally honest, this book started many years ago when my mother first asked me what I wanted to be when I grew up. Even though I was just in kindergarten, I remember telling her that I wanted to be an author. Back then, my response seemed so simple because in my mind all an author did was write. Who couldn't do that? But if I only knew then what I know now. Over the years I've learned that writing is easy because at the end of the day, it does just involve putting words on a page. However, my many years of writing have also taught me that the situations, obstacles, and battles you may endure while trying to put those words on a page can make something that you love to do feel like a heavy burden.

More often than not, because of burdensome situations, I've written with tears in my eyes after being rejected or fear in my heart at the thought of doing something uncomfortable. In these instances, I wanted to push the pause button on life, curl up in my bed, and isolate myself from the world, but something deep inside of me would always say, "Keep writing." So, these words are more than just a nicely written story. This is my journey. A journey full of lessons, mistakes, and wonderful memories. Most importantly, my journey started with purpose and is full of promise. As for you, although your journey may not look like mine, we all were made for a purpose. In addition, God wants everyone to possess his promises. I pray this book guides you to both so you can live a full life.

Acknowledgements

As a first-time published author, I had no clue what it took to produce a well-written manuscript. Therefore, I professionally acknowledge Rose Jackson–Beavers, my book consultant and mentor who helped me on this writing journey.

I'd also like to recognize Dianna Gorden who during the beginning stages of this project, helped me to find my creative flow.

Finally, I would be remiss if I did not include Aaron Houston. He is a wonderful pastor. I thank him for his obedience to God as his spiritual teachings were an inspiration to me.

Introduction

I have a question for you. Why are some of the most attractive flowers found in the wild and rugged terrain? It seems as if these jewels of nature would be better suited as trimmings on a perfectly manicured lawn under the watchful eye of a meticulous gardener. Well, I want to share a very profound, yet simple answer to my question – *process*. All things created on Earth have to endure a process of development. The flower starts off as a seed. With soil, water, and sunlight, it blossoms into God's work of art. By no means is this an easy feat, many flowers are sometimes destroyed by bad weather, grazing animals, and careless human beings who unknowingly and knowingly step on them. Despite these adversities, flowers still grow into what God intended them to be. In the end, their experience in the wild pushes them toward their purpose, which is to reproduce and exemplify the beautiful glory of God.

If you're asking, this book is not about flowers. In fact, what I want to share with you goes a lot deeper. Flowers and human beings share one commonality. That commonality is *purpose*. That's right, I said *purpose*. A flower knows its purpose which is to grow, multiply, and serve as a display of God's earthly glory. I also believe human beings were placed on Earth to grow, multiply, and embody God's glory. In fact, I believe each person has a specific assignment that God has given them in order to accomplish this task. Unfortunately, some people question their existence, which keeps them stuck in the "seed stages" of life. They feel like they have a purpose, but they don't know exactly what it is. These types of people live in survival mode and on a day-to-day basis they let the dirt overwhelm them, weeds choke them, and people trample them into the ground. When this happens, no amount of sunlight, water, or air can help. At that point, only God can revive them so they can grow into their destiny.

If you've ever asked God why you were born, then this book is for you. Or, if you know what you were destined to accomplish but you've been struggling to grow dreams that never seem to flourish, then this book is also for you. After I graduated with an advanced degree, I felt confused because I thought that my purpose was to be a psychologist, but I later on discovered that my degree was never meant to be the apex of my life. No, it was just a tool that God used to push me through dirty circumstances so I could mature into an exquisite flower that exudes godly beauty, intelligence, character, and spirituality. Now that I've grown, I want to help others get past the difficulties of life so they too can reach their full potential.

Scripture tells us, "As long as the earth endures, seedtime and harvest, cold and heat, summer and winter, day and night will never cease" (Genesis 8:22; NIV). This just means that things will always be growing and there will always be seasons. So, if you're the soil, and your dreams are the seeds, the plants are the result of fully matured ideas that have been growing within you. When your destined season comes, the only thing you have to do is trust God, the Master Gardener. He's the only one who can give you godly nutrients that will grow you into the wonderful person you were designed to be. God has the perfect tools to pluck out all of the weeds to help you past the muddy areas of your life. Plus, the Master Gardener has also set aside promises and he's planted them deep within to help you live for him. The time to grow is now! Get ready to reap a harvest of blessings because this is your season.

Comfortable Places

Finally, the moment had come. I walked across the stage with my diploma in hand, feeling like I'd just wrestled a bear, flown to the moon, and discovered a cure for cancer all in a day's time! Of course, none of these things actually took place, but in my mind, that's exactly how I felt. Getting a Ph.D. in counseling psychology was strenuous. To me, it was the mental equivalent of spending a lifetime preparing for the Olympics. After years of shedding blood, sweat, and tears, I accomplished my goal and officially became Dr. Brandy S. Peoples, a psychologist. But as soon as I crossed the stage and took my seat, I noticed something. It was a strange but familiar feeling. I'd felt it before, but I didn't expect to feel it at that moment. What was the feeling? If I could say it plainly, after graduating, taking pictures, smiling, and hugging loved ones, all of my excitement was literally gone.

That's right; my adrenaline peaked, and then plummeted. My anticipation vanished into thin air. Granted, I was still happy and felt incredibly blessed to have the support of my family and friends during what I called *my moment*. But if I were totally truthful, I expected *my moment* to be a little more *momentous*. As I quietly contemplated my feelings, I came to the conclusion something was missing. Although I was an academically accomplished woman, a part of me still felt unfulfilled. Yes, I'd reached a high point of my educational career, but deep down I felt like there was something more. Did I need to set my hopes on another goal? Did I choose the wrong field of study? All I knew was that I felt an emptiness in my life, a void. I sensed the void was leading me to do something different. I just didn't know what it was or when I would begin pursuing it.

What I experienced is called a "short-term high." I'll give you an example of what I mean. Have you ever looked forward to traveling out of town? You start off by researching potential places that you want to visit and then you decide on your destination. Once you're there, you spend the next couple of days in awe. The beautiful people you've never seen before, exotic foods you've longed to taste, rhythmic sounds, and vivid scenery that you've only imagined in your mind, all send you spiraling upwards on an emotional high. But as soon as you think things couldn't be better, your excursion is over, and you're instantly overwhelmed with dread at the thought of going back to work on Monday. That's called a short-term high, and it's something many people can relate to because we're all looking for short-term distractions from our problems.

 **Dr. Brandy S. Peoples**
1 hrs · 🌐

"Short-term distractions will never fill your voids."

We all want answers to our voids. Some people mistakenly use short-term highs to fill empty areas in their lives. One of the most ignored areas happens to be in our spirits. I'll explain. Our voids aren't there by mistake. God has purposely left an empty space in our spirit that only he can fill. As written in John 10:10 (NIV), "...I have come that they may have life, and have it to the full." The spirit is just like our body. It needs daily nutrients to survive. However, unlike the body, the spirit can't be given food or water. It needs something special. Something not tangible. It needs God. Unfortunately, many people don't know this, and they will do anything to fill holes in their spirits left behind by their short-term distractions. In my case, I foolishly thought if I graduated with an advanced degree it would permanently anesthetize my emptiness, but my accomplishments only temporarily numbed it. There was a spiritual hole inside of me, and it could not be filled with academic achievements.

God created us with a spirit that needs him and by designing us in this manner, we will always long for a life full of purpose that only he can provide. Without him, you feel empty. The

2

spiritual emptiness that I felt when I graduated had always been there, I just never knew what it was. For a significant portion of my life, my fulfillment came from setting a goal, and after an intense struggle, it felt so good to achieve what I'd been longing for. During the process, I frequently encountered people who doubted me, so it felt even better to do what the naysayers said I could not do. In my spirit, I had built an elaborate trophy case and I was ready to stock its shelves with what I acquired. No, but all jokes aside, I learned that the more I achieved, the more I wanted, and the more I wanted, the more I realized that my pursuit would be endless.

There was something wrong with me because I never felt spiritually complete. Although I had a relationship with God, I kept trying to fill my spiritual void with accomplishments which was like trying to fill a huge crater with small rocks, my method just wasn't working. From then, I decided I couldn't waste time accruing trophies, especially if they meant nothing to my life's purpose. If I wanted to experience a full life, I needed God to fill my emptiness. First, I had to let go of the silly belief that "trophies" or accomplishments increased my value. Although most of the trophies that I'd wanted were good, I realized God wanted to give me something greater than I created for myself. Something made by him. In the end, I got rid of all the meaningless man-made objects that had little to do with God's plan.

 **Dr. Brandy S. Peoples**
1 hrs

"Accomplishments don't increase your value to God."

Letting go of "trophies" isn't easy because fear oftentimes keeps people stuck amongst worthless things. Merriam-Webster defines fear as *"an unpleasant often strong emotion caused by expectation or awareness of danger."* I would like to add that the origins of fear are just as diverse as its victims. Fear can start early on in childhood or it can manifest in the latter stages of life. For some, the fear of a monster underneath their bed is just as real as the fear of an intruder ransacking their home. Fear can grip you in an instant, chew you up, and spit you out, leaving you traumatized. Fear can also keep people from opening God's gift and cashing in on their blessings. Let's think about it from another perspective. Imagine if a relative of yours mailed you a signed blank check, and the only thing you had to do was write in the amount and then cash it at the bank. Well, our Father has also given us a blank check made available through Jesus Christ. It grants us access to all the treasures of life. Unfortunately, many people are afraid to cash the check. While others don't even know that they have a check to cash. As a result, these people settle for valueless trophies that cannot compare to the real treasure God has in store for them. Thus, fear can keep people immobilized, and though they are standing right at the door of God's treasures, they are too afraid to open it.

Dr. Brandy S. Peoples
1 hr · 🌐

"God has a room of treasures, but some people are afraid to open the door."

The Bible clearly states, "For the Spirit God gave us does not make us timid, but gives us power, love and self-discipline" (2 Timothy 1:7; NIV). This scripture proves that fear does not come from God, but from the enemy. Satan uses fear as one of his weapons of mass destruction because he wants to make sure you're too afraid to let go of the valueless trophies and do something different. Undoubtedly, fear can keep you focused on what seems comfortable. That's why stepping outside of your comfort zone, even if it's for the best, is very hard because no one likes feeling uncomfortable. Satan uses fear because he hopes you will be too afraid to explore opportunities that are outside of your comfort zone. For example, consider how a stay-at-home mom might be too scared to go back to school. Even though pursuing a degree might create wonderful prospects for her family, if she lets the fear of failure or fear of being too successful overwhelm her, she may never experience the blessings God has for her and her household.

4

If God wants to give you a life filled with purpose, then Satan aims to destroy it. John 10:10 (NIV) elaborates on the enemy's goal which is, "The thief comes only to steal and kill and destroy." Satan's attack is three-fold: steal your joy, kill your purpose, and destroy your life. He aims to accomplish these goals through fear and deception. He poisons people with fear, and if that doesn't work, he will blind you with distractions, so you won't have enough time to focus on God. According to 2 Corinthians 4:4 (AMP) "among them the god of this world [Satan] has blinded the minds of the unbelieving to prevent them from seeing the illuminating light of the gospel of the glory of Christ, who is the image of God." The reference "god of this world" only means that Satan has a major influence on secular culture, and he will use anything he can to promote his message of lust, envy, materialism, pride, and violence. All of these messages bring about fear and deception, both are tricks that are as old as time.

Since the beginning, the enemy has been distracting mankind from their purpose and instilling fearful thoughts into our minds all because he wants to keep us focused on things that have nothing to do with God's plan. Everything started in the Garden of Eden. The Garden of Eden was beautiful and full of life. There were all kinds of animals, insects, and plants. At the center of the Garden was mankind. In Genesis 2:15 (NIV) it says, "The Lord God took the man and put him in the Garden of Eden to work it and take care of it." Thus, Adam's assignment was to watch over the Garden and effectively manage all the blessings it would produce. God realized Adam needed companionship, someone whom he could enjoy the blessings with, so God the first surgeon, ever so masterfully removed Adam's rib and formed Eve. At that moment, Eve was birthed into her assignment — to help Adam in the Garden.

Adam and Eve were purposed to live for God. They were full of promise. They also knew their assignment. Plus, they had direct access to the Father and everything he created, so there were no spiritual voids in their lives. But the enemy distracted and manipulated them into thinking that God was withholding information from them because they didn't have access to just *one* thing, the Tree of Knowledge of Good and Evil. God made all kinds of trees. Trees that yielded fruit that were good to eat and pleasing to look at. Even though Adam and Eve could have had any tree they wanted, Satan craftily tempted Eve to eat fruit from the only forbidden tree. Eve then manipulated Adam into eating from the tree. In the end, the master conspirator, Satan, successfully distracted them from their purpose, created a void when there was none, and filled it with fear.

There were no voids in Adam and Eve's lives because they were already like God. Genesis 1:27 (AMP) says, "So God created man in His own image, in the image *and* likeness of God He created him; male and female He created them." Scripture then says, "then the Lord God formed [that is, created the body of] man from the dust of the ground, and breathed into his nostrils the breath of life; and the man became a living being [an individual complete in body and spirit]" (Genesis 2:7; AMP). This proves humans were like God, complete in body as well as in spirit. Adam and Eve didn't have to worry about voids because they were already more than enough. The only missing component was knowledge. God is omniscient while Adam and Eve were not. With this being said, I believe that if they wanted more knowledge, all they had to do was ask God. Nevertheless, Eve attempted to fill a void *without* God's permission. In turn, Adam followed her lead and didn't consider what God had previously told them. Imagine how different things would have been if they had only consulted God first before they let the enemy speak to their fears and distract them from their assignment.

 **Dr. Brandy S. Peoples**
1 hrs 🌐

"Do not entertain distractions because you might lose your position and forget about your purpose."

The enemy's goal is the same today as it was then. Like Adam and Eve, he aims to distract you from your purpose. He also hopes that you'll lose your position in the kingdom. He even

6

anticipates that his efforts will subvert God's plans. But your response determines the enemy's success. Do not allow him to distract you from your purpose which is to live for God. Do not listen to Satan's lies when he tries to keep you from stepping outside of the comfortable places in your life. Do not believe him when he says you are not good enough or God is withholding blessings from you. Do not listen to anything he says. God has already equipped you with everything you need to accomplish your assignment. So, get rid of all those dusty old trophies. Let God restock your shelves with rewards that are worth more than you could ever imagine.

Things to Consider:

Are there things that keep you from stepping outside of your comfort zone? If so, what are they and how can you overcome them to change your situation?

What or who are the "void fillers" in your life? Do they help or hinder your relationship with God?

What are the trophies or idols you put on the pedestals of your life? Write down things that keep you from focusing on God.

Does fear, self-doubt, and insecurity keep you stagnate in life? These feelings come from the enemy. They can hinder your success. To overcome fear, meditate on Isaiah 41:10 (NIV) "So do not fear, for I am with you; do not be dismayed, for I am your God. I will strengthen you and help you; I will uphold you with my righteous right hand."

The Waiting Process

*W*hen you think of the word *wait*, what immediately comes to mind? Well, when I think of the word wait, an image of a waiter pops into my head. While waiting for God, we are also expected to wait on him. Envision a server who waits tables. During their shift, they visually scan the room and actively wait to fill their customers' requests. Whether it is more water, extra napkins, or hot dinner rolls, a waiter can make or break your dining experience. Waiters who serve you with a smile are often given big tips, however the ones who dish out nothing but attitude are never rewarded, furthermore they run the risk of losing their job. While working in the kingdom, we are expected to wait and "serve the Lord with gladness…" (Psalm 100:2; KJV), which albeit difficult, certainly comes with a very big tip which is your assignment in the kingdom of God.

Although being a waiter and waiting are two different concepts, they share one commonality – both involve consistent focus. While waiting, you have to pay especially close attention to the needs of your most valuable customers – the Father, the Son, and the Holy Spirit. By keeping your eyes fixed on these Divine Guests, you become more spiritually aware. Soon thereafter, you'll start to learn what your guests prefer. Does God want water or soda, fish or chicken? I know this sounds simplistic, but I believe that while you're serving God, he's doing most of the work. It may look like you're the only one preparing dishes or clearing off tables, but I can assure you that this isn't so. God is taking care of some major business in the restaurant of life. What he's doing guarantees your success. All you have to do is wait.

A perfect example of waiting occurred when the Babylonians captured the Hebrews. After they were taken into captivity, God instructed the prophet Jeremiah to tell them they would have to endure persecution for 70 years. That's right, 70 years! Although this sounds abysmal, God reassures them by saying, "When 70 years are completed for Babylon, I will come to you and fulfill my good promise to bring you back to this place. For I know the plans I have for you, plans to prosper you and not to harm you, plans to give you hope and a future" (Jeremiah 29:10-11; NIV). Though it isn't directly stated, there is a unique significance to the number 70. Seven represents spiritual perfection while ten symbolizes order and completion in God's laws. From this, it can be assumed that God used those 70 years to teach, develop, and bring about order which can only be achieved through disciplined waiting. Disciplined waiting is what you need if you want to maintain your kingdom assignment.

 **Dr. Brandy S. Peoples**
2 hrs · 🌐

"Waiting is a part of God's perfect plan."

I was slowly introduced to disciplined waiting during undergraduate school. I say this because school is one *long* waiting game. You wait for the end of the semester, then you wait for the end of the year, then you wait until many years pass before you finally graduate. Even after that, you wait until you get certified or licensed. If that isn't enough, then you wait until you find a job. All in all, I spent 12+ years *waiting* to become a psychologist. While you wait, you also have to be disciplined in your studies. This is a lesson that I had to learn the hard way. When I once failed an exam that I didn't adequately prepare for, I went outside to my car and cried in the parking lot. I must've looked like one incredibly sad sight with a runny nose and a flushed face, crying my pain away. Suddenly, in the midst of me wiping away my tears, God said, "But what did I tell you?" At first, I thought I was hearing things. But then I remembered when I took my first human behavior class in high school and fell in love with "matters of the mind," God promised me that I was going to be a psychologist. Just like the Hebrews, he also said no matter how long it takes or how many tests you fail, I have a plan that will come to pass, just

10

wait.

After I gathered myself, blew my nose, and wiped away my tears, I made up in my mind that I wouldn't cry nor would I be embarrassed about superficial failures like not passing tests. I used the word *superficial* because tests and other things like that are indifferent to God. A failed test says nothing about your value. It says even less about God's plans or promises because what he has for you isn't based on your performance. So, when I wiped away my very last tear it felt as if God held a mirror up to my spirit. When I looked into its reflection, I started to see his spiritual perspective of me. I saw that God had earthy treasures waiting, that only I could possess. I was purposed to be prosperous, and whatever assignment God planned would come to pass, as long as I maintained my discipline and obediently waited on him.

The promise of a successful future also applies today, but very few people are willing to wait. Even less are disciplined, and no one wants to be obedient. God reminded the Hebrews, "If you are willing and obedient, you will eat the good things of the land" (Isaiah 1:19; NIV). This is a conditional promise because the word "if" means the outcome is largely based on your actions. For example, *if* you don't do your homework, then don't expect to get a passing grade. However, *if* you do turn in all of your assignments, then you'll pass the class. In God's restaurant of life, he tells people *if* you wait on me, then I'll give you a big tip. But instead of following God's instructions, many "so-called servers" entertain distractions while our most valuable patron is patiently waiting and politely gesturing for their attention. In these instances, God wants us to know that we're not just serving or waiting on him, he in fact is waiting on us. God is waiting to get our attention. So stop entertaining insignificant guests, and learn how to obey his requests. But *if* you're not a willing and obedient server, *then* don't expect God to reward you with your kingdom assignment. This is a promise that's certainly guaranteed.

"If you're not willing to wait, then don't expect to get anything from God."

As I mentioned before, self-examination and seeing things from a godly perspective are key to waiting on God. Early on, I foolishly thought that personal accomplishments made me special, but after I graduated, I didn't feel any more or less valuable. When I failed a very important test, I was forced to take a long look into God's mirror. That is when God spoke to me. He reminded me that a failed test had nothing to do with the inner me because my value was spiritual. Yes, I had flaws in that I was a student with some inconsistent study habits, but that said nothing about who God created me to be, the real me. My spirit was beautiful, intelligent, and creative. I didn't need to pursue external things for validation. All I needed to do was change my focus. When I focused my gaze and began looking into his mirror, God showed me that my spirit was more important, and I needed to work on building that up before I could embark on his promises.

God is a spirit, who communicates spiritually, so it makes sense that he's very concerned about your spiritual growth. In fact, a person's spirit is so significant that John 6:27 (AMP) states, "Do not work for food that perishes, but for food that endures [and leads] to eternal life, which the Son of Man will give you; for God the Father has authorized Him *and* put His seal on Him." Lest we forget, all of our bodies change. We gain weight, lose weight, get sick, get better, grow hair, and lose hair. Your current physical condition may be different from the next person, but all of our ends will be the same — we will all die. This is contrary to what we know about our spirit. Scripture tells us, "and the dust returns to the ground it came from, and the spirit returns to God who gave it" (Ecclesiastes 12:7; NIV). All this means is that lasting pieces of you reside in your spirit, the core of your existence. It will never grow old or die. The spirit is eternal.

12

Since our physical being is temporary, God wants us to focus on our spiritual growth, which will determine our eternal existence. The parable of the Prodigal Son is a perfect example of how an undeveloped spirit (or spiritual immaturity) can cause a person to carelessly destroy God's plans for their life (see Luke 15: 11-32). In this story, a wealthy man had two sons. The youngest son did not want to wait for his inheritance, so he asked his father for a reasonable share. His father granted this request, but the son was immature, and as soon as he was given what he'd been promised, he spent it. When the son hit tough times, he worked as a servant and eventually ended up eating from the pig's trough. Unfortunately, many of us are like the Prodigal Son, and we have to hit rock bottom before we realize that immaturity, irresponsibility, and impulsiveness are the causes of our misfortune.

 **Dr. Brandy S. Peoples**
2 yrs · 🌐

"God wants you to wait because he doesn't want you to mismanage your blessings."

The Prodigal Son lost it all because he didn't want to wait to learn how to effectively manage his blessings. That's what the waiting process is all about. It's meant to develop, refine, and mature your spirit, so when you're given an assignment you won't mismanage it. In 2 Corinthians 3:1, the Apostle Paul tells us that spiritual immaturity can be likened to an infant's eating habits. He considers milk to be the elementary things in Christ while solid food is God's more complex teachings. Infants can only drink milk because they don't have the teeth they need to eat solid food. Or in other words, they are immature. God will not choke you with "meaty blessings" if you are still suckling on milk. For instance, God might want you to invest in the stock market, and if you are to be a success, you'll need a good amount of teeth. He may even want you to open a daycare center, but you can't be dependent on baby food. Your maturity will determine if you get the milk or meat of his blessings, so work on your development.

13

"Do you want a milk or meat blessing?"

Waiting will benefit you and others because God intends to bless vast amounts of people through you. Jesus Christ's entire existence was about blessing others, and even he had to endure a waiting process. Scripture says he was about 12 years old when his parents found him teaching in the synagogue. Then Luke 3:23 (NIV) says, "Now Jesus himself was about 30 years old when he began his ministry." Think about it. Jesus Christ, who was God in the form of a man, waited roughly 18 years before he got started with his kingdom assignment! I believe Jesus did not mind waiting because he used that time to work on his spiritual growth. Had he not done this, it's possible that he might have behaved like the Prodigal Son, mismanaged what he had, and then prematurely stepped out to conquer the cross. Thankfully, Jesus Christ humbly waited while he served the Father, until his death, and eventual resurrection. Now if Jesus Christ had to wait, you most certainly have to wait also.

14

Things to Consider:

Do you have a problem with waiting on God? If so, think about what keeps you from waiting. How can you change it?

If you are waiting on God, do distractions cause you to lose focus? List those distractions and think about ways you can eliminate them.

Oftentimes, we stand in the way of our own blessings. Take some time to self-examine and ask God to show you the areas of your life that need improvement.

Does your kingdom assignment benefit others? If not, think about ways in which your purpose can be used to improve the well-being of others.

Wandering In The Wilderness

*W*henever I travel somewhere unfamiliar, I pull out my cell-phone and use my map application. All I need is a street address, zip code, and name, and I'll make it to my destination. With my computerized map, I do not have to worry about getting lost or nervously asking strangers for directions. I simply drive and wait for my next set of instructions from the automated voice. This type of technology has made traveling so easy that I can only imagine how much better things would be if we could use this to guide us toward our God ordained assignments. Questions such as, who you should marry or where you should move, could be things that you ask. In a flash, the automated voice would give you the answers. No longer would you have to worry about wandering through life or wasting time trying to figure out what you were born to do. Wouldn't life be so much simpler if we all had an app like that?

Of course, I know technology like this does not exist, but I do have another solution that's just as good, if not better. You may have already guessed it. I'm referring to the Bible which is the inerrant Word of God. Without it, we will most certainly end up taking more than a few wrong turns. God, who is infinitely wise, knew his children who were waiting on him for guidance would need something to help them navigate life. So, he gave us the Bible, a road map that highlights the past, directs us to present day truths, and plots a course that outlines the future. What is even more incredible is that the Bible comes with voice operated commands, and when you read it, the Holy Spirit will give you divine instructions. Therefore, if you ever find yourself wandering on an endless course in the wild, I suggest you refer to the Word and the Spirit – a supernatural resource and audible guide that can steer you in the right direction.

Dr. Brandy S. Peoples
3 hrs · 🌐

"The Bible is a supernatural book that can guide you through the wilderness of life."

In my life, there have been many times when it felt as if I was lost and wandering through the wilderness. My most recent experience happened when my residency ended. I had spent years as a student, defended my dissertation, acquired my clinical hours, and after all that, the next step was to secure a job and enter the work force. But when I thought about where I wanted to take my career, I was somewhat afraid and unsure of what to do. When I was offered a fairly reasonable position at a place where I'd been employed, to the dismay of others I turned it down. To say it bluntly, I quit. You heard right, I quit a job long before I started another one. I had a degree that could have taken me anywhere, but I chose a more difficult route in which God led me straight to the "wilderness of unemployment." Some might say I was wandering. I beg to differ because I believed God had something great for me. The only thing I had to do was find it.

Trusting God to lead me to an unknown area of life was difficult because I'm the type of person who likes to plan. I love to make to-do lists, use calendars, and sticky notes to stay on top of things. Nothing compares to the sense of accomplishment I feel when I check off a completed task and move on to the next important job. So when God told me to do something that wasn't on my check list or schedule, I questioned it. Later on, I discovered that God was leading me to a place where I would be completely dependent on his plans and not my own. A place where there were no to-do lists or calendars. A place with no sticky notes. I had no choice but to wait and rely on God. Although I didn't understand what God was up to, deep down I knew he had a special plan, and I had to trust him to

18

lead me there.

I am not ashamed to say, I was confused about who was telling me to quit my job. There were times I'd heard God's voice before, but this time I wasn't sure who was speaking. Was it God or the enemy? If it was God speaking, I did not want to disobey his instructions. If it was the enemy, I had to consider this was a strategic trap set to get me off course. As I prayed each night, I pondered over what I believed God was saying. He then led me to the map that says, "Trust in and rely confidently on the Lord with all your heart and do not rely on your own insight or understanding. In all your ways know and acknowledge and recognize Him, and He will make your paths straight and smooth [removing obstacles that block your way]" (Proverbs 3:5-6; AMP). There was my answer! Up until then, I had been trusting in my own abilities, walking on a path that I'd designed for myself, using my insight to subvert obstacles, and leaning on my own understanding. Now, I was standing on the brink of something profound, and I had to trust God to lead me into the wilderness.

I do not recommend you quit your job without knowing if God is clearly telling you to do so. In my case, God told me to quit, in fact, I'd like to believe my unemployment was a key part of his plan. Oftentimes, God purposely uses the wilderness as training grounds to develop his people. The same thing happened to the children of Israel, who were enslaved by Pharaoh for 430 years (see Exodus chapters 1-15). After Moses freed them, God led them into the wilderness where he performed miracles like parting the Red Sea. God did this and other extraordinary things so when they entered into the Promised Land, they wouldn't doubt his ability. I had to think that if God had a plan for the Israelites, he most certainly had a plan for me. No, there weren't any Red Seas to part, but I had to trust God for a specially designed miracle that would help me pass through my circumstances.

Dr. Brandy S. Peoples
3 hrs · 🌐

"In the wilderness, God has special miracles for you."

The wilderness is not a meaningless experience made for you to wander through. It is a place where God prepares you to be blessed. For example, despite all that God had done for the Israelites, once they got close to their destination, they questioned his abilities. The Israelites were the children of a powerful God, but they still thought of themselves as the lowly slaves of callous Pharaoh. Mentally, they were not ready for the promise. God couldn't allow them to ruin it with their negative thinking, so he let them wander an additional 40 years to transform their minds and prepare them for the blessing that would forever change their lives. According to Deuteronomy 8:2 (NIV), God also used that time, "....to humble and test you in order to know what was in your heart, whether or not you would keep his commands." The Israelites were physically free, but they were mentally enslaved, and spiritually weak. Before they could experience the promise, God wanted them to know who they were so they could carry out what they were called to do.

Dr. Brandy S. Peoples
. 3 hrs · 🌐

"If you don't know who you are, you won't be able to operate in what God has purposed you to do."

The wilderness was used to challenge the Israelites' insecure thoughts about themselves. They were not just any group of people; they were God's children who had special access to his protection and power. Remember this. God does not want anyone to feel insecure, so he uses the desert, another type of wilderness, to challenge our insecure and negative thoughts. In the desert, which is a dry area of life, you will find many lost people who are extremely materialistic or narcissistic. They run after money, cars, and houses. They want others to think they are happy, when deep down they are really insecure. These people are captivated by "stuff" because they think having "stuff" makes them valuable. To maintain their sense of worthiness, they spend years running after things they think are real but are only mirages.

Dr. Brandy S. Peoples
3 hrs · 🌍

"Insecurity and doubt can keep you from your purpose."

The endless pursuit of worldly riches will always keep you running after things in the desert that will only leave you thirsty for more. God never intended for his children to chase false illusions that lead to pride or death. Which is why he uses the wild to teach us the importance of humility. Humility means *modesty*. But all too often, many people who are trapped in the desert are not humble. A prime example of this is Satan. He is the personification of pride. A long time ago, in heaven, Satan believed he would make a much better leader than God. In my mind, I can envision him criticizing God's leadership abilities, and creating doubt in the other angel's minds about the Creator. Ultimately, his prideful campaign turned out to be an unsuccessful insurrection against the Father. After this tragic rebellion, Satan and his companions were cast out of heaven, stripped of their divine purpose, and eternally cursed and forced to forever wander amongst dead things in the hellish wild.

The enemy does not want to wander in the wild alone. In fact, he hopes to tempt others on Earth to follow his same path. He even tried to entice Jesus to defy God's instructions so he could also wander in the wild and not begin his mission. According to Matthew 4:1 (NIV) during Jesus' fast he, "…was led by the Spirit into the wilderness to be tempted by the devil." Scripture then says the enemy tempted Jesus to forgo his fast and eat a piece of bread. He then encouraged Jesus to make a prideful display of his divinity by hurling himself over a cliff and commanding angels to rescue him. The devil even offered

21

Jesus all the kingdoms of the world if he would just submit to him. Fortunately, none of these tactics worked, but it was still a wilderness test Jesus had to experience so he could learn about humility.

Dr. Brandy S. Peoples
3 hrs · 🌎

"Humility will skyrocket you into success. Narcissism will bring you down to your destruction."

While in the wild, I was faced with similar tests that God used to teach me about humility. It happened to the Israelites. It happened to Jesus Christ. It will eventually happen to you. In the end, God told me that my unemployment had only been a part of my wilderness training. After I passed the test, God led me across the hot desert, through the dense trees of the wild, and right into my kingdom assignment. If you want to do the same, let God teach, train, and develop you in the wilderness. A place where he intended for you to pass through, but never to stay and die.

Things to Consider:

Are you in the wilderness? If so, what can be learned during this experience?

What are some ways in which God might want you to improve your humility and obedience to him?

The wilderness is a training ground meant to prepare you for future blessings. What areas of your life do you need to improve before God blesses you?

It's In Your Mind

❧❦❧

*L*et's go on a safari on the wide-open plains of Africa, where gazelles dart through the bushes, zebras sit idly by the water-hole, and majestic elephants stand next to trees as they extend their trunks to eat leafy greens. The scenery is breathtaking. But off in the depths of the wilderness an enemy is watching and waiting. You may not hear or see him, but he's there. Though he longs to fill his belly with you, he's patient enough to wait for a more certain kill. Before you know it, off in the midst, you see a lion! He runs towards you with lightning speed and immediately grips your neck. The pain is intense. You're unable to scream or break free. You feel his razor-sharp fangs ripping through your flesh as you lie in the grass immobilized. Fountains of blood start to emerge from your body to his mouth. You're suddenly cold. Then you feel numb. As saliva slowly drips from his teeth and mixes with your blood, you realize there's no need to fight, so you close your eyes and accept your fate. You faintly drift off into a seemingly peaceful sleep. In the end, you never would have imagined that you'd die on such a beautiful day in the monstrous grips of a cold-hearted killer.

When you decide to venture into the wild to pursue your kingdom assignment, you'll inevitably become a target of the enemy. To better understand my point, let's start at the beginning. In the book of Genesis, God's original plan was for creation to be as it was in the Garden of Eden, where Adam and Eve had dominion. However, the trajectory of this plan changed when Eve was deceived, and then she coerced Adam to consider the devil's cruel plot. Unfortunately, by acting on this, Adam and Eve unknowingly gave their authority over all things to Satan. This did not discourage God, as he is omniscient. He devised a new plan in which Jesus Christ would reinstate God's design. God's children are vital to this plan, so when you decide to take on *your* assignment, you are engaging

Satan in an invisible battle to reclaim your territory.

Dr. Brandy S. Peoples
4 hrs ·

"Satan is the original thief and we are engaged in a battle against him."

Satan won't submit and relinquish what he wrongfully acquired. In addition, he longs to consume what God loves the most – his children. His desire to devour anything attached to God is so menacing that scripture warns us, "Be alert and of sober mind. Your enemy the devil prowls around like a roaring lion looking for someone to devour" (1 Peter 5:8; NIV). Similar to a lion, the devil is a methodological killer with a plan, and he's marked the children of God as targets. Although lions are not the fastest, their ability to wait patiently for their prey makes them ideal killers. To ensure massive fatalities this predator doesn't attack haphazardly. He knows exactly who, what, when, and where to pounce. In fact, this devilish lion stays hidden as he strategically moves toward his next victim. Once he approaches you, he immediately begins a crusade on familiar grounds where if you lose your advantage, all bets are off.

More specifically, Satan wages a spiritual attack against God's children that begins in their minds. If I were to go a bit deeper, the brain is a physical organ that is oftentimes referred to as the "control center" of our bodies. Emotions and behaviors are expressions of thoughts that stem from our brain also known as the mind. It is a complex interaction of our will, perceptions, feelings, and reasoning, all of which makes us who we are. Thus, the enemy's attack against your mind is a direct assault against your entire being because everything we do starts there. One wrong thought can lead to severe emotional and behavioral consequences. So, if the enemy successfully attacks your mind, he can assert his influence over your feelings and behaviors. When he's accomplished this, he maintains what he has longed for all along - dominion and power over you.

26

"Thoughts→Emotions→Behaviors"

Satan wants to corrupt your mind because it is an intangible part of your being with significant intellectual implications. I recently read that the average person has about 50,000 to 70,000 thoughts daily, while a deep thinker may have more than this. Needless to say, we are constantly thinking. Scripture says, "Finally, brothers and sisters, whatever is true, whatever is noble, whatever is right, whatever is pure, whatever is lovely, whatever is admirable – if anything is excellent or praiseworthy – think about such things (Philippians 4:8; NIV). These are the types of positive thoughts that will lead to what God has planned for your life. The devil doesn't want you to think positively because if you do, you'll likely accomplish your purpose in life. So, he tries to distract you with unpleasant, negative, and evil thoughts. If you let him access your mind by whispering lies and asserting his evil influence over you, like Eve, you will have such a distorted view of things that you will not be able to clearly see what God has promised you.

Imagine if just 50,000 of our thoughts were focused on Jesus and other godly truths. This would undoubtedly lead to people living a life grounded on something we are all in desperate need of, knowledge and wisdom. God wants us to have both. Knowledge is needed to get the blessing while wisdom helps us to keep it. Here's an example. Throughout my years in school, I came across a number of extremely intelligent individuals. There were those who never studied but always managed to make straight A's. There were others who were more disciplined who also maintained exemplary grade point averages. Though both were smart, it wasn't a surprise that after graduation many of the casual learners weren't as successful as their hard-working counterparts. In the end, both types of students taught me a valuable lesson. School introduces a person to knowledge but it's up to the individual to apply it to life and better themselves - that's wisdom. You need wisdom if you want to ignore distractions that the enemy will use against you.

Dr. Brandy S. Peoples
4 hrs ⊙

"Wisdom is applied knowledge."

Though I have always considered myself to be a reasonably smart person, I'm not exempt. The enemy is a well-versed assassin and I personally experienced a lot of situations that could've easily been avoided had I only been wiser. Let's consider things from another perspective. The animal kingdom and our kingdom are similar in that ignorance can make you vulnerable to the enemy. Take a lion and a gazelle. Gazelles are fast. They can easily outrun a lion, but they mainly operate on instinct. Although they see other gazelles get attacked by lions, many are not smart enough to prevent their own demise. Now, in no way am I comparing myself to a gazelle, but God says, "My people are destroyed from lack of knowledge [of my law, where I reveal my will]" (Hosea 4:6; AMP). Despite my secular education, the enemy used my lack of knowledge regarding God's will against me. He then led me far away from my destiny and straight to his lair, where he marked me as prey, and then pounced on my circumstances using deception, a deadly weapon in his arsenal.

According to Merriam-Webster's dictionary, deception is defined as, "*the act of causing someone to accept as true or valid what is false or invalid.*" The enemy has mastered the art of deceit. Using this tactic, he convinced me to indulge in seemingly harmless distractions and entertain seemingly harmless people designed to hurt me. It was not immediately apparent, but every distraction led me deeper and deeper into a trap of lies. Satan sets mental traps because he wants to prevent you from fulfilling your purpose and experiencing God's promises. Although he is not omnipresent or omniscient, Satan is a supernatural being. He leads legions of demonic agents that have an assignment which is to attack your mind. These demonic assassins are so skilled in mental deception that you may not even realize you're engaged in a battle between good and evil

28

thoughts.

 Dr. Brandy S. Peoples
4 hrs ·

"So, I find this law at work: although I want to do good, evil is right there with me (Romans 7:21 NIV)."

Like I said before, our brains control our bodies and everything we do starts with how we think. If Satan cannot sabotage your thoughts, he will slither into your heart and try to convince you to focus on your feelings. Why the heart? Jeremiah 17:9 (AMP) tells us, "The heart is deceitful above all things and it is extremely sick; who can understand it fully *and* know its secret motives?" Sometimes our heart has its own agenda, which may be contrary to God's word. For example, one day we can love our spouses and then the next day, despise them. These types of fleeting feelings can manifest in a person's behavior, resulting in sudden shifts. Sometimes "shifty people" will say they love you, but when they *feel* different, they'll contemplate getting a divorce. In this instance, the enemy has managed to get the person to focus on what they feel, despite what God may have said about the reality of the situation. If you act on your heart's feelings, without consulting God, you might lose something that he destined you to have.

Overall, what matters the most to the enemy is your mind. He wants you to think that he wants your house or car, when the reality is, he doesn't need a place to live and he can't drive. I say that jokingly, but these are material objects that he cannot use. Satan has his sight set on something more significant that he wants to possess. Scripture clearly tells us, "So then with the mind I myself serve the law of God; but with the flesh the law of sin" (Romans 7:25; KJV). Simply put, service to God starts in your mind. Which is why Satan wants it. If he manages to successfully infiltrate your mind, then he can act out his evil intentions through your will, emotions, and behaviors. But Satan is not omnipotent. In fact, God encourages us to use the Word to defeat him, which is exactly what Jesus did (see Matthew 4:1-11). Keep in mind, it is what Jesus knew that helped

29

him to prevail, but if you don't know God's Word, you'll be an easy catch. So, if you want to successfully maneuver the devil's mental traps, ask God for wisdom. Otherwise, you are no different from a gazelle that ignorantly drinks from the same waterhole where other gazelles are ruthlessly slaughtered by lions, day after day.

Things to Consider:

The enemy doesn't have any new games, just different players. To guard against a future attack, think of things he's done in the past to hurt you. Once you have identified them, outline some strategies that will help you to stand against him.

How has the enemy tried to prevent you from pursuing your kingdom assignment? During these times, consider how it affected you mentally, emotionally, and physically.

Identify some of the deceptions and distractions that the enemy tries to confuse you with. Search out Biblical truths to counter his lies.

Remember. What God says is more important than how you feel. Ask yourself, are your behaviors based on your feelings or God's truths?

Scripture says the enemy is *like* a lion, which means he is posing as something that he is not. With this in mind, how has the enemy tried to scare you? List ways to overcome your fear.

Faith Is The Substance

I love to eat cookies, brownies, donuts, and any other sugary treat that you can name. As a child, I can remember watching my grandma, Fay, bake bread pudding, peach cobbler, and chocolate cake, all from scratch. Over the years, I have eaten my fair share of treats and I can honestly admit that my grandmother's baked desserts tasted a whole lot better than the premade sweets I've bought from the grocery store. My craving for these tasty delights once motivated me to whip up some desserts just like my grandma but after looking up several recipes, I realized I needed to follow a specific set of instructions. Realistically, I don't have that kind of patience. Even the most novice cook knows that in order for things to taste just right, you have to take the necessary time to stick to the recipe — the substance of any good baked treat. Just like eggs, milk, and baking soda make up the batter of a delicious red velvet cake, faith is the substance of all the good things that we can expect from God.

First off, before we can get a clear understanding of faith, let's start by discussing what substance means. Merriam-Webster defines substance as, "*the essential nature,*" or the "*ultimate reality that underlies all outward manifestations and change,*" or even the "*physical material from which something is made, or which has discrete existence.*" Scripture tells us "Faith is the substance…" (Hebrews 11:1; KJV). Before we go on, understand that faith is not just *a* substance, meaning one of many. No, faith is *the* substance, the material from which something is made or exists and it is vital to how you live for God. If I were to go back to my discussion about delicious treats, undoubtedly the batter of a cake is essential to how it tastes. It doesn't matter what type of pan, oven, or the perfect temperature you bake it at, if you forget a key ingredient of the batter, your cake may not taste right. When you consider this, it is fair to say that though it may be gooey, uncooked batter is very important because it is the fundamental staple of the cake. It makes the cake what it is. The substance is the batter and baking it in the oven only helps it to taste better. If I were to apply this to people, God has already given you "the substance" which is everything you need to accomplish your goals. Although you might not feel ready, the pressure from "hot" situations is a part of the process that only makes you better.

Dr. Brandy S. Peoples
6 hrs ·

> *"You are the substance. God has already put everything in you that you need to accomplish your dreams."*

Since we've established that faith is the substance, which I likened to a tasty cake, I'd like to discuss the rest of the verse where it states, "Faith is the substance of things hoped for..." For as long as I can remember, I've always had hopes that seemed too big for me. Since kindergarten, I hoped to one day become an author. Then in high school, I hoped to become a psychologist. After I graduated, I hoped to find a job in a specific area of study. Needless to say, there are other things that I'm still hoping for, and while in pursuit of them, I've experienced a lot of "hot" events. One such situation occurred when I was driving home on the first day of class during my graduate studies. I was in a three-car accident. A vehicle hit a truck, which then rear ended my brand-new car, and almost pushed me into a busy intersection. Oh, and how could I forget, on that day it was raining so badly that I could barely see the road. This situation caused me a lot of pressure and stress, but I held on to my hope that God could use it to make me better.

Faith was the substance of my aspirations to pursue a doctoral degree. I couldn't let obstacles deter me from that goal. Though I looked like a nervous wet mess standing by the side of the road in the rain, after I assessed the damage to my vehicle, I began to think about the promises God had made to me. He promised I would become a psychologist, and I was in the

34

final stretch of my journey. Yeah, it was raining. Yeah, I also felt alone. And yeah, my reality did look somewhat doubtful, but my faith was fortified. There was no way I was going to let a small dent on the back of my car and a little bit of neck strain stop me. The dent could be fixed. The pain in my neck was minor, but my dreams were a part of an eternal plan. The same can be said about your kingdom assignment. Do not let a temporary situation change your mind about what you have been praying for.

 **Dr. Brandy S. Peoples**
5 hrs 🔾

"God has his oven set at the perfect temperature, so you won't burn up."

By now, you should know that faith is the substance of things hoped for, and if I were to say it simpler, faith is the base of what you are anticipating from God. Let's address another more complex aspect of faith. The rest of Hebrews 11:1 (KJV) says, "…and the evidence of things not seen." Some other similarly related words for evidence are *proof, data,* and *facts.* Things not seen are *intangible objects that cannot be visually perceived.* The Amplified Version of the Bible says, "Faith comprehends as fact what cannot be experienced by the physical senses." This means that faith is the belief in and assurance of the spiritual realm.

God is a supernatural being who exists outside of energy, time, matter, and space, the physical properties of our world. God reigns in heaven, which is in a spiritual dimension far outside the boundaries of human understanding. When God issues a command, it first manifests in heaven, where he resides. The outcome of his order takes place in the natural, which is Earth. However, because we cannot see anything happening, we sometimes doubt what is taking place. That's when we have to rely on our faith in God to help us understand things beyond our comprehension. God is doing something supernatural which human beings reap the benefits of because it first happens in heaven, and then it transpires on Earth.

A wonderful manifestation of the supernatural occurred when a foreign army, intent on killing the prophet Elisha, surrounded him. Elisha's servant was frantic, so he calmly prayed, "Open his eyes, Lord, so that he may see. Then the Lord opened the servant's eyes, and he looked and saw the hills full of horses and chariots of fire all around Elisha" (2 Kings 6:17; NIV). Though Elisha could not see all that was happening, he had faith that something was being done. God had ordered a supernatural army from heaven to assist him in a battle on Earth. That's what having faith in the evidence of things not seen is all about. Know that God is always working behind the spiritual scenes of your life and just because you can't see him, doesn't mean he isn't there. So, if you find yourself in a place where it seems as if your dreams aren't going as planned, know that at any given moment, God is ready to give you a glimpse of his heavenly army that will triumphantly lead you into victory.

Dr. Brandy S. Peoples
5 hrs · 🌐

"Have faith that another reality exists."

Faith is so significant that scripture tells us, "And without faith it is impossible to please God, because anyone who comes to him *must believe that he exists* and that he *rewards those who earnestly seek him.*" (Hebrews 11:6; NIV emphasis mine). First off, you must believe in God. Some people have a hard time with this because they wonder how God could let bad things happen in this world. My answer to that is, evil atrocities such as murder, sex trafficking, extreme poverty, and any other horrible thing that you can name can be traced back to Satan, who is the "god of this world." The enemy does have some rule over Earth. He has infiltrated a good majority of it and its inhabitants with his lies, tricks, and deceit, all of which will lead to death and destruction. But this says nothing about God's existence or his perfect plan. Furthermore, it is not up to us to figure out how God uses the devil's handiwork to bring about his will. We are only encouraged to depend on our faith, which determines how we perceive reality.

"God is the Ultimate Authority over Earth."

Job is a perfect example of how faith can set your reality. Job was good. He was also wealthy, but his life suddenly shifted when God mentioned his character to Satan who then asked God if he could challenge Job's faith. God knew Job's heart, so he allowed Satan to test him by killing his animals, servants, and children. During this test, Job lost everything, but he still refused to turn his back on God. In the midst of it all, he simply responded, "…the Lord gave, and the Lord hath taken away; blessed be the name of the Lord (Job 1:21; KJV). Satan was furious. This made him want to bring Job down all the more. The enemy was then allowed to attack Job's health, and he became so sick that even his wife said he should, "curse God, and die" (Job 2:9; KJV). Time went on and things got worse, Job's friends suggested he had caused his own misfortune. But through everything, Job maintained his faith which he humbly demonstrated by praying for the people who criticized him, his friends. Immediately after, Job's situation improved and God blessed him with everything he lost, plus more.

The moral of this story? Bad things can happen to good people. Even though Job experienced so much loss, he did not let his unfortunate reality influence his perception of God. Without knowing the cause of his suffering, Job still kept his faith. In fact, even when he was in physical pain, Job prayed for his friends. This brings me to another great lesson, have faith and take the focus off how you feel. God is omniscient and omnipotent, which means that he is all-knowing and all-powerful, and he is the only one who can use the pressure from life's heavy situations to bring about his blessings. So, when you're going through personal issues that seem to have no end, keep your faith in God. He knows how much you can endure.

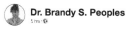 **Dr. Brandy S. Peoples**
5 hrs · 🌎

> *"Faith should be based on what you know and not*
> *what you feel."*

Like Job, Jesus Christ, "the author and finisher of our faith," (Hebrews 12:2; KJV) was also a good person who had done no wrong, yet he was falsely imprisoned, tortured, and left to die an agonizing death. Through it all, Jesus relied on his faith and focused on his assignment — to save mankind. In fact, he was so focused on saving others that he prayed for his captors and even comforted a repentant thief as he hung on the cross in excruciating pain. As for you, you might also be a good person, and while trying to accomplish your dreams, you may experience some painful moments. Nevertheless, if you want to be a success, have faith in God who is the only one with a supernatural, panoramic view of life. Have faith in what he sees, and let that shape your perception of reality.

Things to Consider:

Is it difficult for you to live by faith? If so, how can you change it?

Evaluate your prayer life. Do you believe God for the impossible? Or do you pray for ordinary things to occur in your life?

Does fear outweigh faith in your life? If it does, what makes you afraid? How can you alleviate these fears?

James 2:17 (NIV) says, "…faith by itself, if it is not accompanied by action, is dead." How can you put your faith into action?

Reminder: When you find yourself in the middle of a challenge, scripture says you should be "[looking away from all that will distract us and] focusing our eyes on Jesus, who is the author and perfecter of faith [the first incentive for our belief and the One who brings our faith to maturity]" (Hebrews 12:2; AMP).

Trusting God's Plan

*B*y high school, I had my life perfectly planned out. I knew I wanted to go to college, then attend graduate school, make a ton of money, get married, and finally have children. It was almost as if I'd created the perfect movie in which I was the director, producer, screenwriter, production designer, and leading actress. Now that I have lived through a significant portion of my film, I can honestly say things have not gone as planned. During my movie, some of my supporting cast members have been fired. I've made last minutes changes to the set which has been moved several times. There have been some production delays. New scenes have been written. Others were deleted and then ripped into shreds. And on more than one occasion, I have forgotten my lines, which has forced me to go back to the script.

As you can see, there will always be problems during the production of your own picture. Some issues are easily resolved, while others will be much harder to figure out. Nonetheless, I've realized that when you're making your life's movie, things will always come up. So it is okay for me to embarrassingly stumble over my words or uncomfortably act alone because it's all a part of the process, and right now, I'm refining my craft. Therefore, I try not to spend too much time worrying about my lines or looking for someone to star alongside me. God is the Creator of my movie and he most certainly has a solution for all of my mistakes and more. We are his actors with only one job — trust the script he's written.

God's script is essentially his plan for our lives. He has written everything down from beginning to end. In the opening scene he writes, "Before I formed you in the womb I knew you [and approved of you as my chosen instrument], and before you were born I consecrated you [to myself as my own]; I have appointed you as a prophet to the nations" (Jeremiah 1:5; AMP). This means that before any of us were born, God wrote an individual script for every person that has ever lived. Although the circumstances behind the conception of your script were outside of your control, God has always been in the director's seat with his pen and pad running the show.

In the beginning of God's script, he wrote in whom you would be born to, where you would be born, your gender, your race, and everything else that makes you who you are. We all start off as novice actors and actresses, so as the movie goes along, God purposely pairs us with other trained professionals that will help us to master our skills. Also, he has written a wide array of situations and put them in the script so we can practice before we act out our purpose. If you make some mistakes, it's okay. God is the best acting coach and he's ready to teach us discipline, wisdom, and patience. So finally, when the movie premiers, your character will stand out from the other untrained actors, and it is a role that only you can act out.

 **Dr. Brandy S. Peoples**
6 hrs · 🌐

"Trust what God, the Author of your life story has already written."

I *love* movies. I'm the type of person who loves movies so much that I don't mind going to the theater by myself. From fantasy, crime drama, science-fiction, and action adventure, all of my favorite films have extremely intriguing characters. The main character of films is usually the leading actor or actress, also known as the protagonist. This person's role is more developed in that you know their background, strengths, and weaknesses. During the movie, the protagonist typically acts in the most scenes and faces the most challenges. In fact, their character is so well written that you feel connected to them. Their victories feel like your victories. Their struggles are your struggles. By the end of the film, the protagonist eventually overcomes all the things that held them back and you walk out of the theater, feeling a sense of pride.

If you have not guessed it by now, we are the protagonists in God's film. As the protagonists, we will all face distinctly different obstacles. Some of them will cause you to question decisions you have made, thereby leading you to doubt your abilities. Others might weaken your faith and you might consider quitting the movie. Don't worry though. All of the best actors have experienced doubt or a loss of faith. When this happens, always refer to the original script, the Bible. In it, God encourages us to say to him, "I do believe; help me overcome my unbelief!" Personal crisis or issues in your life are difficult, but necessary parts of the acting and movie making process. However, you should never forget that you are the protagonist and while you are in the midst of an emergency, God has already written a strategy for your success.

As the protagonist, a personal issue I had to face that made me question my success was singleness. While filming, I have acted in several scenes without a male co-star, which at one point made me feel like there was something wrong with me. After I reviewed the continuous film footage of me on dinner dates alone or at home on a Friday night watching television, I questioned God's directorial skills. I wondered what type of movie he was making because mine was really boring. I can laugh at it now, but singleness once bothered me because I had bought into the lie that a relationship validated my existence. When I asked God how to handle it, he told me to go back to the script which said, "For I know the plans I have for you declares the Lord, plans to prosper you and not to harm you, plans to give you hope and a future" (Jeremiah 29:11; NIV). This changed my entire perspective. My relationship status or lack thereof, was part of a larger, more prosperous plan. So instead of focusing on singleness, I needed to rely on God to get me through these seemingly boring scenes so I could make it to the next part of the film.

Dr. Brandy S. Peoples
8 hrs ·

"What seems boring to you might be the beginning of an action-packed adventure."

As an actress in God's movie, I had to trust that singleness was a role I was destined to act out. Maybe God didn't want me to have a male co-star at this point in the movie. No, it was not the easiest role to accept but God never promised that we would like everything written for us. Nor did he promise that every role would be easy to portray. Personally, I would have preferred to play the role of a married, rich woman, who shops all day. But I had to consider that God had another plan in mind when he decided to write next to my character's name – single, psychologist, and minister. Also, as a reminder, he wrote in the script, "Trust in the Lord with all your heart and lean not on your own understanding; in all your ways submit to him, and he will make your paths straight" (Proverbs 3:5-6; NIV). Right then, I decided that no one could play this role better than me. Maybe my purpose, which is to live for God, would be better fulfilled as a single person. Most importantly, I had to trust the Divine Writer because if God put it in the script, it was because he wanted to use it to make me into a star.

 Dr. Brandy S. Peoples
6 hrs · 🌐

"If it's in the script, God wants to make you a star, but you won't accomplish anything if you insist on doing things your way."

Some people either don't like or don't trust God's script, so they write their own narrative. But because they lack God's skillful insight, they don't understand how one simple change in the script can bring about a chain of events that can ruin their destiny. For instance, when God asked Jonah to go and warn the Ninevites of impending doom, he adamantly refused by running away. He didn't think the Ninevites were worthy of redemption (see Jonah chapters 1-2). Instead, Jonah developed a new script for himself, which included getting on a ship that was set for a place outside of God's plan. But because God wanted his movie, and not Jonah's, to eventually come to pass, he brought about a unique set of circumstances. Jonah was thrown overboard, swallowed by a big fish, and then trapped in the belly of that fish for three whole days before he accepted the position God wanted him to play. When the fish spit Jonah out, he finally took center stage in Nineveh to perform the rest of his role.

The story of Jonah shows us that no matter how much you try to avoid acting out God's roles, if it is in the script, it will eventually become a part of your movie. Keep in mind, what God has planned does not always sound appealing, but your faith in who he is should help you to understand that he is a writer who does not make mistakes. Furthermore, God will not force you into acting out your part. Certain things, he will let you do on your own. This is referred to as the permissive will of God. However, he hopes you will choose his way and act out his plan, which is called the perfect will of God. If you decide against it, you'll likely face unfavorable circumstances (like Jonah) that God will use to bring about his preferred movie ending. It is best to accept what God has originally written, because your narrative cannot compare to the perfect plan he has put together for you.

Dr. Brandy S. Peoples
6 hrs · ✿

"God's perfect production is tied to his divine will."

Though God has wonderful plans, trusting what he has written can be extremely difficult because of his unique way of doing things. Remember, God is a supernatural being with no limitations, so what he does may not make sense to mere mortals. For instance, it sounds silly for God to trap Jonah in the belly of a big fish. In fact, this doesn't even sound like a real situation. But whenever you are confused or struggling to understand things, God encourages us to go back to the script, which says, "For my thoughts are not your thoughts, neither are your ways my ways, declares the Lord" (Isaiah 55:8; NIV). As the writer and director, God doesn't need our approval for what he does or doesn't include in his film. He has complete creative control over everything. It may not make sense to us, but if he wanted a big fish to trap Jonah, then what he wants will happen.

Another primary component of movies are the supporting cast members. A co-star supports the lead actor or actress in many ways. For instance, if it's a love story, the co-star may be a romantic interest. If it's a thriller, the co-star might be a person who terrorizes the protagonist. In either situation, it can be said that co-stars play a fundamental role in the story and are essential to the main character's development. Over the years, I've had a lot of supporting cast members who have helped me and others who have hindered me. The ones who helped always ended up playing reoccurring roles in my life, while the ones who hurt me were eventually cut from the film.

Understanding who needed to go versus who needed to stay was a skill that took some time to master. Although I don't have much of a problem with it now, poor casting decisions made parts of my movie unbearable to watch because on many occasions, I made someone a series lead when they should have only had a guest role. These individuals didn't have the skills needed to carry the film, and their bad performances caused me to act outside of my character. In my movie, a couple of bad actors took me from "calm" to "crazy," and before I knew it, they shifted the entire direction of my film. These people had to get cut before they ruined what God intended to be a blockbuster.

Dr. Brandy S. Peoples
8 hrs ·

*"Just because you start a scene with a person doesn't
mean they'll stay with you throughout the film."*

If we were to go back to God's script, he has written about
plenty of people who also chose bad cast mates. Samson is a
Biblical character that comes to mind (see Judges chapters 13-
16). Samson was a Nazirite who God blessed with supernatural strength. In return, God wanted him to maintain a disciplined life. The stage was perfectly set, and Samson's movie
could have been a heroic tale. However, the movie turned into
a conspiracy film when he told Delilah, a supporting actress,
that his hair was the secret to his strength. Delilah then told
the Philistines, the antagonists of Samson's film. Subsequently,
they captured him, cut his hair, and gouged out his eyes. After-
wards Samson prayed, "…Please God, strengthen me just once
more, and let me with one blow get revenge on the Philistines
for my two eyes" (Judges 16:28; NIV). In the final scene, Samson was able to kill the Philistines, but his movie could have
lasted a lot longer had he not chosen Delilah, a background
character, and turned her into his leading lady.

Some people don't realize that everyone wasn't meant to act
alongside them. In Samson's case, he foolishly chose a background character or in other words, an extra. In a movie, we
don't know anything about the extras because they aren't essential to the lead actor's character. The audience never knows
their names, they don't have speaking parts, and most of their
traits aren't fully developed. Essentially, their character, role,
and position is limited. In Samson's movie, Delilah should
have remained an extra because of her undeveloped character traits. But Samson was so captivated by her beauty that he
looked past all of her flaws. Also, he did not even realize that
she had made other attempts to set him up. I guess Samson
must have missed the part of the script that reads, "Charm is
deceptive, and beauty is fleeting; but a woman who fears the
Lord is to be praised" (Proverbs 31:30; NIV). In movies, the
best-looking character may in fact be the devil in disguise.

47

Though Delilah looked good, she was a questionable actress who did not possess godly character traits. First off, the script says that Delilah accepted a bribe from the Philistines, so we can assume that she was manipulative. Then it tells us Samson fell in love with Delilah, it says nothing about her falling in love with him (see Judges 16:4). From this, we can also assume that Delilah took advantage of Samson's feelings and used them against him in her deceptive plot. Take note, while pursuing your dreams there will always be beautiful or handsome cast members who will want to be on the center stage in your movie. They'll start off as sweet, but God only knows their real intentions. If you entertain them, they will try to change the direction of your movie so you will be unable to pursue God's plan for your life.

Dr. Brandy S. Peoples
6 hrs ·

"Bad decisions can turn a drama into a horror story."

Another main character of a movie is the antagonist. The role of the antagonist is to strongly oppose the protagonist. In many films, the protagonist and antagonist are often depicted as having an early connection, then suddenly something happens that causes a break in the relationship. From that point, nothing is the same and the rest of the movie is spent with the two of them being at odds with one another. In our movie, the antagonist is Lucifer, and in the prequel, he was created by God to be an, "...anointed cherub who covers" (Ezekiel 28:14; KJV). Things changed when Lucifer boldly declared, "...I will be like the Most High" (Isaiah 14:14; KJV). Lucifer became even worse when he convinced the other angels to rebel against God and then, "...he was cast out into the earth, and his angels were cast out with him" (Revelation 12:9; KJV). As a result, his character's name changed from Lucifer, which means morning star to Satan, the adversary.

Though originally given a perfect role, Satan became an egoistic actor who thought he would be better off as the director. Even though he may have convinced some of the other angelic actors to defy God, he did not achieve his primary goal – he wanted to write, produce, and direct the heavenly film. Because of his actions, Satan was stripped of his anointing and forced to play the villain, a lesser role than what he was originally given. Now Satan is furious. He and all the other ousted angelic actors have decided to boycott God's movie. He hates the other angels who did not rebel with him. Satan loathes the Director. And if you think his animosity couldn't get any worse, Satan despises all the human actors and actresses because we have access to something he no longer possesses – eternity.

In the end, some actors will continue into eternity where they will be cast in a heavenly role. But, the devil's ending is fatal, he will burn in the lake of fire, and will not be allowed to return for a sequel (see Revelation 20:10). If he can't have all the best roles or return for a sequel, Satan doesn't want anyone else to either, so he tries to sabotage your earthly acting. Plus, he will do everything he can to keep you from reading God's script. If you do read it, the enemy hopes you will forget your lines, quit acting, or not understand what is written in it. His overall goal is to convince you to boycott God's film, just like he did, so you can suffer his same fate. If you don't read or understand what's in God's script, you will never know that you should, "Submit yourselves therefore to God. Resist the devil, and he will flee from you" (James 4:7; KJV). The role you are meant to play involves having authority over the devil.

Dr. Brandy S. Peoples

"Read the script. You have power over the enemy!"

Whether it is preventing an alien invasion or capturing a murderous serial killer, all movies need a character who exemplifies bravery in the darkest of hours. God has written a fantastic story that would be meaningless if there wasn't a hero. Jesus Christ is the star of God's film. In fact, the only reason why we have been given the roles we're currently playing today is because of how he defeated the enemy and saved the

49

day. It goes without saying, the stage on which you and I will act out God's purpose sits on the foundation of Jesus Christ's heroism. And when you trust God's plan, you are giving credit to the champion of all of our lives, Jesus Christ. For that reason, you need to read the script and rehearse your lines, so you can act out your purpose. If you do, in the final scenes of your life, you will meet the hero who made it all possible.

Things to Consider:

Since our lives are part of a film that God is directing, what role do you think you play? The protagonist acts according to God's plan. The antagonist goes against God's plan. Which one are you?

Sometimes it can be hard to fire people who you think are significant to your film. How has the inability to "let go" negatively affected what God has planned for you?

Like Jonah, have you rejected a role that God created for you? What was the outcome of your decision?

In God's film, there are characters that are meant to be the stars while there are others who play background roles. How can you prioritize your relationships to better fit this concept?

God's Character

*L*et's not forget the most important character in this film of life — God. While other people are meant to play specific parts, God is the only one with multiple roles, and he knows *exactly* what they are. He is the writer, producer, director, and most importantly, the Creator of everything. Nonetheless, despite God's authoritative position, some people are still confused about the part he plays in orchestrating the plans that he has for their lives. They also wonder if they can trust God to direct situations that will lead to their dreams coming true. When this happens, God encourages them to go back to the script and learn his character, line for line. The script is an extension of God, and his character description reads, "God is not human, that he should lie, not a human being, that he should change his mind. Does he speak and then not act? Does he promise and not fulfill?" (Numbers 23:19; NIV)

Though the first line of God's character description reads, "God is not human," don't mistake that to mean he isn't real. God is *not* a mythological character or ghost in the sky. God is "not human" because he is more than a man. God is so complex that scripture says, "I make known the end from the beginning, from ancient times, what is still to come. I say, 'My purpose will stand, and I will do all that I please'" (Isaiah 46:10; NIV). This is a powerful statement because it confirms that God knew exactly how things would end in the beginning when he created this world. I know this sounds confusing, but all you need to know for now is that God is not limited by time or other constraints such as the past, present, or future because he exists outside of them. Before creation came to be or you were born, God predestined your purpose, kingdom assignments, and special blessings. Right now, God is waiting for you to learn more about his character so he can show you how to apprehend what he put in place for you a long time ago.

Dr. Brandy S. Peoples
7 hrs · 🌐

"Don't worry. God knew how things would end at the beginning of time. He has everything under control."

While other people might lie or make vows that they never intend to keep, God is the complete opposite. Throughout the Bible he makes a point to reveal divine aspects of his character and remind us that he is different from humans. This is referred to as *theophany*, a Greek word meaning *visible manifestation of God*, either in *human* or *non-human form*. To display his holiness, God appeared to Moses in flames of fire from a burning bush (see Exodus 3:2), God later says, "Do not come any closer. Take off your sandals, for the place where you are standing is holy ground" (Exodus 3:5; NIV). During another encounter with God, Moses asked to see his glory, God told him, "you cannot see my face, for no one may see me and live" (Exodus 33:20; NIV). He then tells Moses, "When my glory passes by, I will put you in a cleft in the rock and cover you with my hand until I have passed by. Then I will remove my hand and you will see my back; but my face must not be seen" (Exodus 33:22-23; NIV). And just from looking at God's back, Moses' face shone so much that when the Israelites saw him they became afraid. These supernatural manifestations further affirm that God is not a human, therefore it is impossible for him to lie about your destiny.

Trusting God because he is a divine entity who cannot lie is a difficult concept to grasp because human beings are limited to the natural realm. God is an uncreated eternal being. There was never a time when God didn't exist, nor will he ever have an end. Thinking of it this way, it is nearly impossible to accurately explain a supernatural entity using natural terms. For example, Exodus 3:13-14 (KJV) is one of the earliest introductions of God. It is a scripture that shows how challenging it can be to describe him. In this text, Moses asks God exactly who and what the Israelites should refer to him as. God first says,

"...I AM." He then goes on to describe himself as, "the Lord and God of your fathers" (see Exodus 3:15). I believe God first wanted to let the Israelites know there are no words in any lexicon to describe him so just say, "I AM." Ultimately, God's character cannot be confined to a word, simple phrase, or restricted to any language. "I AM," is God's way of saying, I am more than your human mind can ever conceive. "I AM," is the power behind all creation. "I AM," is the reason why you have a purpose. "I AM" is self-existent.

Dr. Brandy S. Peoples
7 hrs ·

"God is the great I AM. He is more than you can imagine."

When I was a little girl, I was extremely inquisitive about the "GREAT I AM." I had always heard that God was there in the beginning, but clearly someone must have birthed him? And if he did have parents, who were they and where did they come from? There had to be an answer, so I asked my grandpa Leon who was extremely wise. He told me there were some things I would never figure out, with this being one of them. To this day, I still don't quite understand where God comes from, but I can honestly say I don't think it matters. Until we get to heaven, all we need to know for now is that God is an eternal spirit. What's much more important is God's character because if you want to receive his blessings, you should establish a relationship with the one who blesses.

One of the most significant aspects of God's character is his Spirit. God is not physically present to lead us towards our goals, so he talks to us through his Holy Spirit. God's Spirit was there when you were born. God's Spirit will be there when you die. The Holy Spirit "will never leave you or forsake you" On the days in between, the Holy Spirit wants to assist you in every area of life. (Joshua 1:5; KJV). The Spirit knows about the overwhelming feelings of insecurity that stem from daily disappointments, and he longs to empower you. The Holy Spirit also understands the emptiness people feel when they lose a loved one, and he hopes you will let him lovingly comfort you while you are grieving. You cannot see God's Spirit. You have to trust that he's there. When you finally realize God's Spirit is omnipresent, you will let him ease your fears during your darkest of hours and lead you to victory on your most successful days.

We are made to be solely dependent on God's Spirit because if he does not exist, then we would not exist. When we cry, God understands. When we are happy, God also celebrates with us. God knows all that we are going through because we were designed to be in a relationship with his Spirit. In fact, God possesses one of the most universal character traits that strengthens our bond, and that is love. From babies to hardened criminals, everyone desires love. Some describe love as a tingly feeling when their spouse comes around. While others think love is a byproduct of the neurotransmitter oxytocin, and when it is released you feel a surge of positive emotions. My definition may not be as clear, but for me, love feels like a warm spring day mixed with joyful moments shared with my family and friends. However, you choose to describe it, love is by far the strongest of all emotions and according to scripture, "God is love" (1 John 4:8; NIV). Love comes directly from God, so if you do not understand him, you are likely to misunderstand love.

 **Dr. Brandy S. Peoples**
7 hrs ·

"God is love and the Holy Spirit is our loving guide through life."

Keep this in mind. Because God is not human, his expression of love is not the same as what we see in people. For some of us, love might mean endless compliments or an intimate dinner by candlelight with our spouse or significant other. But God's love is sacrificial and is best described as, "For God *so loved* the world that he gave his one and only Son, that whoever believes in him shall not perish but have eternal life" (John 3:16; NIV emphasis mine). According to this scripture, love takes place when you give up all that you have for another person. Plainly put, love involves sacrifice. When you show this type of love, God will unlock the doors of his treasures for you. How do I know this? Well, when God gave his only Son, the doors of eternal life were opened to us. Therefore, the sacrifices that you make for others just might be the key that unlocks God's door to his purpose and promises for you.

You might be asking, what does love have to do with my purpose? I'll tell you. If you want to own a business, you will need love. When you have love, you'll be kind to your employees. If you want to be successful, you will also need love. Love will help you to understand that you can't mismanage your blessings especially if it compromises or hurts others. Galatians 5:22-23 (AMP) says, "But the fruit of the Spirit [the result of His presence within us] is love [unselfish concern for others], joy, [inner] peace, patience [not the ability to wait, but how we act, while waiting], kindness, goodness, faithfulness, gentleness, self-control." Notice, how love is mentioned first while the other characteristics follow. This means that the evidence of God's Spirit is love, the unselfish concern for others. Love marks the beginning of your purpose and if you have it, you will have everything else.

 **Dr. Brandy S. Peoples**
7 hrs · 🌐

"God's character is love. If you have it, you will treat everything with care."

Unfortunately, many people ignorantly pursue unofficial replicas of love manufactured by the adversary. Satan is not an originator but a counterfeit artist who produces goods similar to what God has already developed. This copycat has successfully duplicated a version of love called lust. Interestingly enough, both love and lust are described as an *"intense longing"* or *"deep desire"* for *something* or *someone*. But to distinguish God's love from Satan's lust, refer to the scripture, "Love is patient, love is kind. It does not envy, it does not boast, it is not proud. It does not dishonor others, it is not self-seeking..."

(1 Corinthians 13:3-5; NIV). Love is made by the Creator, and it comes with a warranty put into effect by Jesus Christ and sealed by the Holy Spirit. Lust is an unauthorized copy of love that has been smuggled into existence by an illegal dealer who does not have permission from the manufacturer, nor has he paid the cost to produce quality work.

 Dr. Brandy S. Peoples
7 hrs

"There is a significant difference between love and lust. Love is measured by what you give up. Lust is measured by selfish gain."

I have a funny personal story that better explains my point. Once, I bought what I thought was a perfect looking knock-off purse. I was so excited about my new bag that I purposely carried it on my way to a restaurant in a somewhat affluent area. Words couldn't express how I felt as I proudly walked down the sidewalk with my purse perfectly draped across my torso. But in an instant, the straps suddenly snapped! What once was a beautiful looking purse was now oddly dangling from one side of my body to the other. I was embarrassed. The quality of the purse did not match my lofty expectations. On that day, I learned a valuable lesson. When you settle for something that is not authentic, at any moment, what you think is firmly holding it together, can instantly break.

Only God's love is authentic. Unfortunately, some people settle for knock-off versions that are bound to fall apart (like my purse) because they don't know the difference between love and lust. The Biblical story of the Woman at the Well is a perfect example of this (see John 4:1-29). In this text, Jesus Christ meets a Samaritan woman at a well, she was thirsty for water. But as the story goes on, we learn that the Samaritan woman was also emotionally thirsty for love. She had been settling for cheap versions of lust and had gone from relationship to relationship, looking for, but still never finding the real thing. When she stopped by the local well, she didn't expect to experience what she'd been looking for her entire life, and that

58

was Jesus. He was not interested in flirting, no he offered her something much more. Jesus wanted to quench her thirst for love with living water which flowed from his personal well.

Dr. Brandy S. Peoples
7 hrs ·

"If you pursue lust, you will always be thirsty."

Just like the Woman at the Well, there are a lot of thirsty people who will do anything just to get a sip of what they think is love. Here's what I mean. A woman who is thirsty for a sip might purposefully have a child with an unfaithful man because she hopes he will lovingly commit to the relationship if they start a family together. Let's not forget there are also dehydrated men who cater to inconsiderate women because they think it will eventually lead to their girlfriends accepting their hand in marriage. These types of thirsty people are wrong. Without love you probably will not have any joy, peace, faithfulness, kindness, or anything else related to it. So it's silly to settle for a relationship built on a poor substitute that will never quench your thirst for the real thing.

Dr. Brandy S. Peoples
7 hrs ·

"God is pure love while the enemy only offers lust that is tainted by sin."

God wants us to experience "living water," which is pure love that adds purpose to and lengthens our lives. "Dirty water," or lust which is offered to you by the enemy, will never satisfy. Yet, people willingly reject unlimited cups of God's pure *agape love,* just so they can drink temporarily from Satan's dirty toilet. I know it sounds disgusting, but I believe it hurts God to know that some of his children are so thirsty for love that they do not even realize they are drinking Satan's dirty water called lust. But God is love and he loves you. He wants to give you large amounts of his pure water. If you decide to drink, the amount of toilet water you've had thus far, won't matter because his water will instantly rejuvenate you. Because of his character, God won't force you to drink what he or Jesus Christ offers, he wants you to lovingly choose, since love is who he is.

Things to Consider:

How do you think of God? Is it possible you have limited his abilities based on your restricted notions of him?

Have you ever settled for cheap versions of love? If so, how did those experiences affect you? What can you do to heal from them?

Think about this. God is love and I believe Jesus Christ is a human manifestation of it. If a person wants to experience real love, they have to get to know Jesus Christ.

In my experiences, I've discovered that relationships motivated by lust do not last long. Think about your past relationships. How does your loving relationships compare to the ones motivated by lust? Remember, lust isn't just about physical desire. It's possible to lust after wealth, fame, attention, status, and a host of other things.

Relationship Over Religion

*W*hen I was a girl, my mother made me, and my younger sister go to church religiously. On Wednesday, we had Bible study. On Saturday, we had youth and adult choir practice. Then there was early Sunday school. After Sunday school, we'd go into morning worship service. There were also afternoon services we attended, as well as prayer meetings, annual days, and gospel concerts. As you can see, I went to church a lot. These church experiences were wonderful because from them, I learned some fundamental truths about how we should reverence God, respect our elders, and carry a tune while singing, or at best, blend in with the people who can. But as I got older and faced different trials, I realized there was something missing. My childhood experiences taught me a lot about church culture, but very little about how to establish a relationship with God.

Church culture isn't necessarily a bad thing. Every organization has a set of traditions and principles they practice, and if healthy, they can bring about love and unity amongst the people. For example, some people worship during the week while others attend services on the weekend. Neither of them are better or worse. But if your mind and heart are not centered on God, what day you worship on or how many church services you attend will not matter. Let's think about it from another perspective. Although it may be a nice gesture, no married person wants their spouse to say, "I love you," three times a day, every day, if they don't mean it. They could even scream it from the top of a mountain, but if there is no authenticity to it, the other person will not be moved. The first part of Romans

12:9 (NIV) says, "Love must be sincere." Larger-than-life repetitious displays of emotion do not mean anything if you're not sincere. One soft whisper of "I love you" from a person who sincerely cares is enough to send chills up and down your spine. Simply put, screaming, "I love you," will not get you any closer to God.

Dr. Brandy S. Peoples
8 hrs ·

"Screaming, 'I love you God,' won't convince him to move on your behalf."

Establishing a relationship with God is important because he is the only one who can lead you to your purpose. Although we all share the same general purpose which is to glorify God. Each of us was uniquely made to carry out God's purpose in very special ways. For instance, one distinct aspect of my purpose is ministering the Word of God. Now, I want to be honest with you. Becoming a minister was never at the top of my "to-do" list. At the time, I thought that I was too young to minister. Plus, I had not been to seminary, so I felt unqualified. Given these concerns, I wrestled with the idea for a while, and then I tucked it away in the deep crevices of my mind. I left it alone, but as time passed I couldn't ignore the gentle tug on my heart to teach God's people. At some point I realized that I had to make a decision because if God wanted me to become a minister, I did not want to forfeit his plan for my life.

I had a dilemma that needed to be solved, so I had to go to God. At that moment, I remembered my grandfather, Mr. B.T., who at the close of our annual family reunions in Mississippi would fervently pray for our safe return back home. His prayers were so sincere, and I believe God heard him, so I decided to pray for an answer. In fact, scripture tells us, "This is the [remarkable degree of] confidence which we [as believers are entitled to] have before Him: that if we ask anything according to His will, [that is, consistent with His plan and purpose] He hears us" (1 John 5:14; AMP). So, I prayed like never before. I listened to worship music, I cried, I read scriptures, I verbally prayed, I wrote prayers down, all in that order. Before I knew it, hours had passed but it didn't matter to me because I was willing to do whatever it took to hear from God. When God answered, it felt as if the Holy Spirit was all around me. At that moment, I accepted my call into the ministry. I was finally at peace.

While praying, I had a spiritually intimate moment with God who exists as himself, Jesus Christ, and the Holy Spirit. We, his creation, are also triune. We have a spirit, and a soul, that resides in a body. God cannot relate to us physically because he is not a physical being. He can't always communicate through our emotions (which is part of the soul) because scripture tells us, "The heart is deceitful above all things, and desperately wicked: who can know it" (Jeremiah 17:9; KJV). God, our Creator, wants to talk to our spirit. Genesis 2:7 (NIV) says, "Then the Lord God formed a man from the dust of the ground and breathed into his nostrils the breath of life, and the man became a living being." In the Hebrew language, the word for spirit is *ruah,* which means *wind* or *breath.* God's breath is what comprises our spirits. It's the only part of our existence that comes straight from him.

 **Dr. Brandy S. Peoples**

"Spiritual intimacy is necessary if you want to develop a relationship with God."

Essentially, a spiritual relationship is a three-fold union we share with the Father, the Son, and the Holy Spirit. Each of them plays a unique role. Scripture says, "For there is one God and one mediator between God and mankind, the man Christ Jesus" (1 Timothy 2:5; NIV). This means that God talks to Jesus Christ about our purpose, who then instructs us on what we need to do to fulfill it. God does not want us to misunderstand his plans, so he speaks directly to our spirits, the purest part of our existence. We are also encouraged to pray "in Spirit and in truth," (John 4:24; KJV) for answers about our divine destiny. When we do this, we are simply blowing back on the Creator what he originally breathed into us, his Spirit. The Father wants to bond with us in this way because we are the only creatures on Earth with his Spirit, and Jesus Christ's sacrifice made it possible for the Holy Spirit to talk directly to us. Therefore, spiritual intimacy is paramount to initiating a relationship with God.

When I was struggling with the idea of becoming a minister, long hours of praying and reading scriptures were ways that I got past my body and soul and tapped into my spirit to ask God for an answer. If I were to visually describe these states of being, I would use a circle with three rings. On the outer ring is the physical, and because we will eventually die, this is a temporary condition. Our emotions or soul makes up the inner ring, which is comprised of our mind and will. This is where we experience things such as free-will, romance, determination, and fear. These emotions can be short-term or long lasting, they are subjective experiences and they aren't always based on God's truth. Then there is the spirit, which lies at the center of the circle. Since God is a Spirit and we best connect to him spiritually, this is where spiritual intimacy takes place.

Praying, is a spiritually intimate act. We are also encouraged to "pray in the Spirit on all occasions with all kinds of prayers and requests..." (Ephesians 6:18; NIV), which means having an uninterrupted conversation with the Trinity. I'll explain. Because Jesus Christ had a human experience on Earth, he can relate to your humanity. So, when you pray, he expresses your human needs to the Father on your behalf. The Father then sends the Holy Spirit, who is omnipresent, to soothe and comfort you. Here's an example. When I was unemployed, I prayed to God. Of course, he's never been unemployed but "your Father knows what you need before you ask him (Matthew 6:8; NIV)." Because Jesus Christ, our Advocate, is one with the Father, he understood my earthly needs. Throughout my prayer, I could feel the Spirit encouraging and reassuring me. Although I didn't get a clear answer about when my unemployment would end, the Father, Jesus Christ, and the Holy Spirit told me that eventually everything would be alright.

Dr. Brandy S. Peoples
8 hrs ⦿

*"The Trinity; God, Jesus Christ, and the Holy Spirit
work together as a team to guide you throughout life."*

Church is just one of the places where you can pray to and experience spiritual intimacy with God. In the Book of Exodus, God established the first church or in other words a tabernacle where he could commune with the Israelites (see Exodus chapters 36-39). God gave specific instructions. First, he wanted the outer court of the building where commoners could offer sacrifices. Then he wanted an inner court, also called the Holy Place, where only priests could enter. Third, there was the innermost court, the Holy of Holies where the Ark of the Covenant and the Ten Commandments would be held. Most importantly, the innermost court was the dwelling place of God's Spirit. Only the high priest could enter, and once a year they would go into the innermost place, through the veil, which kept regular people from crossing into this sacred court.

Back then, intimacy with God was an arduous task because all of these steps had to be followed in perfect order. Plus, imagine having to enlist the services of a high priest, and then wait a full year before he could enter into the innermost court and pray to God on your behalf. These rigid religious customs did not promote spiritual intimacy; therefore, Jesus Christ was sent to initiate a different way of doing things. This is what he was talking about at the well with the Samaritan woman (see John 4:1-29). Essentially, he told her that although you're accustomed to worshipping God in a geographical location, the time has come for you to worship with your heart *and* mind. Jesus Christ was the beginning of a new way of worship, and when he sacrificed his life, he broke the veil between God and mankind. Now everyone has access into the Holy of Holies where God's spirit resides.

"God isn't concerned about a building. You are the tabernacle he wants. Worshipping him begins in you."

Now, we all have unlimited spiritual access to God through prayer, meditation, or reading the Bible. Yet some people still think that their relationship with him is solely dependent on their church membership. If I were to explain it another way, simple church attendance can be likened to the outer court of the tabernacle in that it's only the *first* step in establishing a relationship with God. Now don't get me wrong, church is a great place to fellowship with other believers, but if you are not spiritually intimate with God while there, you might as well be marked as absent. God is not interested in checking attendance, and tardiness is not much of a concern. While you're in church, God mostly wants to deepen the loving relationship that the two of you share so you can more intimately worship him.

If you want to experience a deeper level of intimacy, then you need to go to the inner court or in other words, tap into your emotions, which is the *second* step of your relationship with God. Trust me, God wants to hear all about how you feel because his Spirit is the Comforter. But do not stay in your feelings because there is an even greater level of intimacy to experience — the Holy of Holies. This is the third court and metaphorically the *third* step of your relationship with God. In this place, God helps you focus on things that are bigger than how you think or feel. In the innermost court, you get to experience God's Holy Spirit. The Holy Spirit can show you mysteries about your life which will lead to your purpose and his promises.

Unfortunately, many people in church never experience the innermost place with God's Spirit. Why? Because they have been deceived by Satan who has led them to believe that all they need to do is just show up for church. Of course, he doesn't want you to worship God, "in Spirit and in truth" because this is the deepest level of intimacy and he wants you to be a spiritually empty person who believes all of his lies. Furthermore, the enemy knows that when you pray from this innermost place, the Holy Spirit will ease your fears, fill your voids, and lead you to your godly purpose. Don't get me wrong, going to church is great because you get to fellowship with other believers, but if you don't experience God's spirit or truth while there, you haven't really worshipped him. This is why I believe Satan gets really upset when you have an intimate worship experience with God while you are at church.

Dr. Brandy S. Peoples
8 hrs ·

"There are too many people in church that are physically present but spiritually absent."

To prevent true worship at church, the enemy likes to keep people focused on minor issues like what you are wearing to service, so you will stay in the outer courts of intimacy. If you do make it to the inner court of worship, the enemy will then try to get you to focus on your feelings. He doesn't mind if you *feel* like you're in God's presence without you actually entering the Holy of Holies. Finally, if you make it to the innermost court and hear from the Spirit, the enemy will attempt to overwhelm you with doubt. While in the innermost court, he can't stop God from speaking but he can confuse you about what you heard. To trip people up he will ask you, "Did God really say?" If you doubt God's Word, then the enemy has accomplished his goal. In this instance, I can see Satan and his imps giving each other high fives because they've successfully used doubt to keep another one of God's children from having a truly intimate moment with God that will lead to them fulfilling their purpose.

69

Dr. Brandy S. Peoples
8 hrs · 🌐

"Ignore the enemy when he asks, 'Did God really say?"

Though it was not directly mentioned, there is a significant association between God, mankind, and intimacy. When Adam and Eve defied God's orders, disobedience entered into the world, along with other evil atrocities such as murder and hate. Because God cannot abide with evil, his Spirit (which is pure) took residence in a building where you had to pass through three courts just to experience him. God did not want his children to have these long-term worship limitations. Therefore, Jesus Christ, a physical representation of God, was sent as a sacrificial offering so we could pass through the outer physical and inner emotional courts. When he rose on the third day, he broke the veil so we could enter into the third court, which is the spiritual Holy Place. If you have not noticed, all of this involves the number three. The number three signifies divine completion. Jesus Christ completed a divine task so we can experience physical, emotional, and spiritual intimacy with the Father, the Son, and the Holy Spirit. If you want to experience what God has for you, pour your body, soul, and spirit into establishing a relationship with him to completely fulfill your whole purpose.

Things to Consider:

Since we discussed the three-fold nature of man, what do you think your relationship with God is mostly focused on: emotions or spirit?

As stated in the scripture, we are to worship God in spirit and in truth. Have you had a spiritually intimate experience with God? If so, think about what you did so you can incorporate this into your daily life?

Is your spiritual relationship with God at the top of your to-do list or do you value other things more?

Think about this: Worship is necessary if you want to fulfill your purpose.

The Three-fold Nature of Man

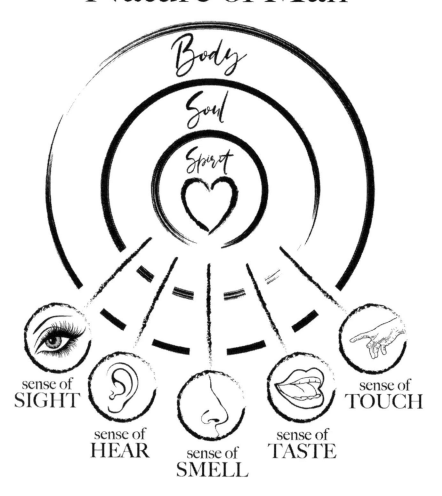

Body

Soul

Spirit

sense of
SIGHT

sense of
HEAR

sense of
SMELL

sense of
TASTE

sense of
TOUCH

Authority and Power

✤✤✤

*O*nce, my cousin playfully told me that my legs looked like baseball bats. I was a young, insecure kid, so instead of brushing it off as a joke, I shriveled up like a wilted flower. From that point on, I did not want to wear any skirts or shorts. My grandmother, whom we affectionately called Ma' Dear, always knew what to say to make things better. So I felt so good when she later said to me, "Child, look at those big pretty legs!" At the time, her loving praises helped me get past my insecurities but when I became an adult, my childhood doubts surfaced again. Some years later, I found myself asking, "was I good enough?" Even as a grown woman who many considered to be beautiful, likable, and intelligent, I sometimes thought of myself as just a cute nerdy girl who wore red glasses with "baseball bat" looking legs. I couldn't get these childhood insecurities out of my mind. I felt inadequate, and self-doubt kept me from realizing that I was special.

This story sounds familiar because in the beginning, Adam and Eve also underestimated themselves. If I were to further explain, God made them distinct when he said, "Let us make mankind in *our* image, in *our* likeness (Genesis 1:26; NIV emphasis mine). First off, Adam and Eve were not typical human beings. They were made in the spiritual image of God and physical likeness of Jesus Christ. They were the picture of beauty. Scripture then says that God made them, "so that they may *rule* over the fish in the sea and the birds in the sky, over the livestock and all the wild animals, and over all the creatures that move along the ground" (Genesis 1:26; NIV emphasis mine). Rule means to *govern* or *control*. Usually, monarchies are the only institutions in which kings and queens rule over the inhabitants of a kingdom. In a monarchy, you are born a prince or princess. When you become an adult or get married, you take on the title and responsibilities of a king or queen.

Unfortunately, Adam and Eve did not realize that they didn't have to wait to sit on a throne to claim a kingdom. They were already the royal authorities who were created to rule.

 **Dr. Brandy S. Peoples**
9 hrs · 🌐

"Mankind was created to rule over a kingdom."

According to Genesis 1:1 (NIV) it says, "In the beginning God created the heavens and the earth." Then something happened. God saw "the earth was formless and empty, darkness was over the surface of the deep" (Genesis 1:2; NIV). Because God has a plan for everything he creates, he miraculously transformed the Earth into a kingdom. God didn't need it for himself. He resides in heaven and he would rule creation from there, but "the earth He has given to the children of men" (Psalm 115:16; AMP). This new kingdom was meant for Adam, Eve, and all of their descendants. After the new planet was formed, all of God's creation would stretch from the deep blue sea of the natural realm, pass the starry skies, darting through the unknown areas of space, and right into the supernatural realm of heaven. Our kingdom was limited to the Earth, but God's creation would be limitless.

The earthly kingdom that God created for us was made different in every way. The Earth is the only place in the known universe that was habitable. This is not a coincidence. The Earth was specifically designed for us and at the center of it was the Garden of Eden, the most picturesque garden ever created. The Garden was also exceptional because God's Spirit dwelled there with Adam and Eve. I can only imagine what his Spirit looked like in this place. In my mind, I picture it as a brilliant light bouncing off of the leafy greens, landing on the tropical colored fruits, illuminating exotic animals, and then settling on the shimmering blue water. Finally, in the midst of all these incomparable creations, I see his Spirit, as clear as a diamond, radiating off of his royal descendants. The Spirit's presence in the Garden of Eden was the evidence of Adam and Eve's lineage, because of it they didn't need crowns.

As royalty, Adam and Eve were given clear instructions, take authority over the Earth, starting with the Garden of Eden. For example, one of their first orders was to, "Be fruitful and increase in number; fill the earth and *subdue* it" (Genesis 1:28; NIV emphasis mine). Subdue means to *overpower* or *subjugate*. Adam and Eve were supposed to take authority over the Earth, but they were also ordered to overpower it. No doubt, God could easily have done this himself, but he wanted his children to take responsibility for their own earthly kingdom and experience the benefits of ruling for themselves. Plus, God wanted to institute a new type of government on the Earth, and his royal descendant's actions would determine its success.

God wanted Adam and Eve to play a distinct role in implementing a type of governmental order called a *theocracy*. Under this system, God would operate as the spiritual authority who issues commands from heaven, and then he would put someone in position on Earth, so they can carry out his divine orders there. If correctly followed, his orders would flow from the supernatural to the natural realm. Ultimately, God aimed for his will to be accomplished, "...on Earth as it is in heaven," (Matthew 6:10; NIV). In heaven, there is order. The angels aren't wandering around aimless hoping to stumble on something to do. They are sure about their purpose. They anticipate God's promises. And most importantly, they play their position. Heaven is perfect because the angelic beings abide by the governmental order. God wanted to bring this picture of perfection to Earth, but it was up to Adam and Eve to follow the theocratic order.

Dr. Brandy S. Peoples

"God is the spiritual authority of a theocracy."

God did not force Adam and Eve to obey his orders. When he entrusted the kingdom to them, he also gave them free will. God told them, "You are free to eat from any tree in the garden; but you must not eat from the Tree of the Knowledge of Good and Evil, for when you eat from it you will certainly die" (Genesis 2:16-17; NIV). That's right, Adam and Eve were given the ability to freely choose between different courses of action. They were presented with a good and bad option. This is what a loving Father does; he gives his children choices and he makes them aware of the consequences. But an evil dictator rules a dictatorship where people are forced to submit. God is not an evil dictator. He wanted Adam and Eve to freely choose the theocratic order which would have made their kingdom perfect.

 **Dr. Brandy S. Peoples**
9 hrs · 🌐

"Free will is one of God's greatest gifts to mankind."

Adam and Eve could have eaten from any tree, yet they chose to eat from the only tree in the Garden of Eden that God specifically warned them about. This is because they were manipulated by a slithering snake who concocted a plan to take their kingdom. Let's not forget, Satan and the other angels who didn't want to follow the theocratic order, were cast out of heaven onto Earth as punishment (see Revelation 12:9). I can only speculate, but it's possible that after Satan was cast down to Earth, he likely ruined it. Which explains why it was left void and full of darkness. God then transformed the decimated remnants of Earth into a dwelling place for his royal descendants. As for Satan, he was still on Earth but he had to submit to the new king and queen. The enemy couldn't stomach the thought of him bowing down to anyone, so he had to quickly think of something. His plan, he convinced Eve to eat from the forbidden tree which changed the governmental order. In the end, Adam and Eve ended up yielding to a commoner of their kingdom, an entity they were told to rule over.

Adam and Eve did not realize they were being manipulated into submitting to a lesser creature they were supposed to overpower. God told them, "...And to all the beasts of the earth and all the birds in the sky and all the creatures that move along the ground—everything that has the breath of life in it—I give every green plant for food" (Genesis 1:29; NIV). Essentially, God gave them authority and power over all the things on Earth, which included Satan. But when they broke the theocratic order, they corrupted the system by taking orders from the enemy, instead of God. As a result, their royal status was taken away, they were forced out of the Garden of Eden, and they had no choice but to venture out into the wilds of the Earth as paupers in a strange land.

After Satan stole the kingdom, God orchestrated another plan to get it back. He told the enemy, "Because you have done this, cursed are you above all livestock and all wild animals. You will crawl on your belly and you will eat dust all the days of your life. And I will put enmity between you and the woman, and between your offspring and hers; he will crush your head, and you will strike his heel" (Genesis 3: 14-15; NIV). Essentially, God told him that in the future, he would send someone to restore what was stolen. And there was only one person who could do it. He'd been there in the beginning. He'd be there in the end. Most importantly, he was willing to follow the theocratic order which was the only way to successfully maneuver the devil's traps. Of course, God planned to send Jesus Christ to Earth, "to save that which was lost" (Matthew 18:11; KJV). Adam and Eve lost the authority and power they once had over their kingdom. Jesus Christ was sent to restore it.

Before Christ's entrance into the Earth, Satan, without hesitation, perverted everything about the stolen kingdom. His ultimate goal, rule with force and then kill all of what God created. In just a short time, Satan manipulated Cain into killing his brother (Genesis 4: 8), infected humanity with wickedness before the flood (Genesis 6: 5), and to appease his evil cohorts, the devil even convinced people to sacrifice their own children (Psalm 106: 35-38). Years passed, and God had grown weary of seeing his royal descendants suffer under the rule of a tyrannical king who brought only poverty, disease, and death into the world. What was meant to be a magnificent empire, the devil quickly turned it into something horrendous. This ruthlessly evil, counterfeit king had ruined all aspects of humanity, but his rule over the Earth was never meant to be long-term. Jesus Christ was soon to come.

In another part of the kingdom, John the Baptist, eagerly anticipated and prophesied about the Savior of the earthly realm, Jesus Christ. He often declared, "Repent, for the kingdom of heaven has come near" and "Prepare the way for the Lord" (Matthew 3:2-3; NIV). When John finally met Jesus, he baptized him. Soon thereafter, a dove rested on Jesus' shoulder, and from heaven God said, "This is my Son, whom I love; with him I am well pleased" (Matthew 3:17; NIV). This was a remarkable event. The dove represented the Holy Spirit, and when it sat on Jesus' shoulders, God had given him power to begin his mission. His orders – restore the kingdom. Immediately, Satan knew his rule over Earth was coming to an end. So he went back to his bag of tricks, and he hoped to pull out something lethal to use against Jesus. But Satan's games are all the same. His plan, Satan offered Jesus the stolen kingdom and all of its riches, but with one catch. Jesus had to submit to him! Or in other words, break the theocratic order (see Matthew 4: 1-11). Jesus was too smart for Satan's childish antics. He keenly maneuvered this trap using God's Word. Jesus had bigger things to deal with because there was something more important at stake.

Jesus listened to God, and he successfully overcame this final trap. He was ready to reclaim the kingdom and made his mission known by saying, "The Spirit of the Lord is on me, because he has anointed me to proclaim good news to the poor. He has sent me to proclaim freedom for the prisoners and recovery of sight for the blind, to set the oppressed free" (Luke

4:18; NIV). The oppressed were Adam and Eve's descendants. Although many years passed, God had not forgotten about them. They were burdened by poverty, sickness, and worst of all, death. Let me explain. God originally created the Earth to be like heaven, where there is no death. But when Satan stole the earthly kingdom, he injected an evil order into the world, and at the center of it was death. Death was the most consistent weapon in Satan's arsenal. Death was merciless. Death was fatal. There was no prejudice with death because no one could escape it. That includes dogs, cats, plants, insects, birds, fish, everything. And of course, that includes mankind. He planned to use it to destroy all of God's creation. Jesus Christ wanted to free mankind *and* dethrone Satan, using one of his own weapons against him, and that was death.

Dr. Brandy S. Peoples

*"Jesus' goal was to set the captives of the kingdom
free from death."*

Freeing Adam and Eve's descendants wouldn't be easy. In many ways, they preferred bondage over freedom because they had grown accustomed to the heartless ways of the world. This made it difficult for Jesus to set them free. The sleeping royals had forgotten their lineage and had been behaving like ordinary citizens. Jesus had to do something extraordinary to get their attention. So, he miraculously healed the sick, fed the hungry, and taught all that would listen about the good news of God's kingdom. He wanted to show Adam and Eve's descendants what royalty really looked like. But still, Jesus had to do something about death. It had been lingering above the Earth like a dark cloud, and he had to get rid of it. The only solution – sacrifice his life. That's right. Jesus Christ had to do what no one had done before. And when he died and was resurrected on the third day, Jesus defused death, the enemy's primary weapon. Though we are still destined to physically die, Jesus' sacrifice brought life to our spirits. Then, when a person died, they were also spiritually separated from God. Now, because of Jesus' sacrifice when a person dies, our spirits will continue into eternity.

In the end, Jesus triumphed over death and the kingdom was restored. I can almost see him confidently storming in the room where the enemy had been nervously sitting on the throne and without hesitation, snatching the keys of death away from him. After Jesus Christ was resurrected, he said to his disciples, "All authority in heaven and on earth has been given to me" (Matthew 28:18; NIV). Much later in scripture, one of his disciples, John had a vision where Jesus boldly declared, "I am the Living One; I was dead, and now look, I am alive for ever and ever. And I hold the *keys of death* and Hades!" (Revelation 1:18; NIV emphasis mine) In the Bible, keys are a symbol of authority. When a person is given a key, it means they have the right to open or close something. Think about it. If I give you the keys to my house, that means you to have *total access*. Jesus' keys were not ordinary, they were special. And because he possessed a set of supernatural keys, he had complete access to everything in God's kingdom, which included life *and* death.

Now it was time to wake up the kingdom's slumbering citizens who had been wandering as nomads with no purpose or plan for their lives. Jesus Christ had given them a kingdom, but they needed the right tools to access it. Jesus Christ told his disciples, "I will give you the keys of the kingdom of heaven; whatever you bind on earth will be bound in heaven, and whatever you loose on earth will be loosed in heaven" (Matthew 16:19; NIV). But that promise wasn't just for them, he wanted his disciples to show others how to access the kingdom. Jesus Christ used his key to close the door of death, and now he wanted future kingdom citizens to use their key to unlock the authority and power of the reclaimed territory they had been given.

The privilege of using the keys of authority and power of this divine kingdom, are only for citizens who obey Jesus Christ. If you follow his commands, Jesus also assures, "I have given you authority to trample on snakes and scorpions and to overcome all the power of the enemy; nothing will harm you" (Luke 10:19; NIV). The "snakes and scorpions" is a metaphor for Satan. He's not a literal snake but he first manifested in the Garden of Eden as one. Now that his cover has been blown, he masquerades in a variety of ways and he rules from a dark kingdom that is not easily perceived. From this kingdom, he lurks in the crevices of self-doubt, puts on a prideful charade, poses as rebellion, and feeds off your fears. He also commands legions of demons with evil abilities. Some are skilled in trickery; others are experts of violent acts. But when you have the keys of authority and power, you can lock the door on the devil and his imps, and there is nothing he can do to break free.

 **Dr. Brandy S. Peoples**
8 hrs · 🌐

"Disobedience killed a kingdom.
Obedience restored it."

Obedience gives you access into the kingdom. Once you're inside its gates, you become a kingdom citizen. As proof of your citizenship, you're given keys of authority and power. If properly used, these keys will unlock your godly purpose and promises. That's why the devil tries to manipulate you into disobeying God and thus, handing over the keys to the kingdom. If you give Satan the keys, you will not have the authority or power to evict him because you willingly let him in! Not to mention, when you let Satan in, you're changing the governmental order by giving a lesser being the keys to the kingdom. And because Satan likes to rule, he will eventually take over, without you even knowing it, and before long you will forget your royal lineage. But remember. *You* are a member of a royal priesthood. *You* are seated in heavenly places with Jesus Christ. *You* were meant to rule over Satan. *You* were meant to possess the keys that unlocks your purpose, authority, power, and promise.

81

Dr. Brandy S. Peoples
9 hrs · ⊠

"When you submit to the enemy, you're giving him
authority and power over you!"

The kingdom of God isn't about a physical place on Earth. Like I said before, the kingdom of God stretches from the depths of the sea to other unknown areas of the world. You are one of many unknown areas, so God's kingdom is about *you!* God wants you to become an ambassador of his supernatural government. When you submit to him, another portion of his kingdom gets built within you, and Jesus Christ becomes Lord over it. However, when you purposefully defy God, you are submitting to Satan who wastes no time gathering bricks to begin building his dark kingdom inside of you. So, if God orders you to open up a business, write a book, or go back to school, do it! His commands come from heaven and he wants you to carry them out on the Earth. Trust the order. God wants to use your gifts to recruit new citizens who will continue to build his kingdom.

Things to Consider:

Have you ever underestimated your abilities? If so, think of how this fits right into the enemy's plan, so you won't maximize your potential. How can you build your esteem and confidence?

Remember. Jesus Christ has already given us authority and power to overcome challenges. In order to access them, you have to submit to his leadership.

Think about this: If you are not a citizen of the kingdom of God (adhering to Jesus' rules of government and order), then you are by default a citizen of the opposing kingdom of darkness.

Scripture to remember: 1 Peter 2:9-10 (AMP) "But you are a chosen race, a royal priesthood, a consecrated nation, a [special] people for God's own possession, so that you may proclaim the excellencies [the wonderful deeds and virtues and perfections] of Him who called you out of darkness into His marvelous light. Once you were not a people [at all], but now you are God's people; once you had not received mercy, but now you have received mercy. "

Possessing Your Promise

✻❀✻

*T*hroughout the scriptures, we can see that God loves to make promises. By definition, a promise is a *commitment or covenant between two people where one person assures the other that a particular thing will occur*. For example, if your partner gives you a promise ring you assume you will get married. Even though you might experience relational difficulties, like arguing about what you want to eat for dinner, it pales in comparison to what matters the most, your relationship. And when you look down at your hand, your ring reminds you of your beloved's promise. Once you are engaged, all the insignificant arguments disappear like a vapor in the air, and in its place, you focus on your enduring love. Finally, on your wedding day, after you have taken your vows, you realize the trivial disagreements or awkward arguments were just minor bumps on the road. Your wedding ring is the proof of a promise kept.

Believe it or not, the Bible is full of promises. God makes promises not because he likes to hear himself talk, but because they are part of a much bigger plan. The very first promise is recorded in Genesis 3:15 (KJV), when God says to the serpent, "And I will put enmity between you and the woman, and between your seed and her seed; he will bruise your head, and you shall bruise his heel." This statement is referred to as *proto-evangelium* which means the *first mention of the good news of salvation*. The serpent manipulated Adam and Eve into sin, and this particular scripture shows us how God planned to right their wrongs. Although they couldn't ignore the consequences of what they did, the good news was that God promised to send Jesus Christ, the Savior. He would restore the authority, power, and salvation to the citizens of the formerly lost kingdom. The first promise in the Bible, also turned out to be the best promise, and the end result outweighed any mistake Adam and Eve could have made.

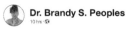**Dr. Brandy S. Peoples**
10 hrs · 🌐

"God's promises are part of a bigger divine plan."

Take me for example. God promised that I would be a psychologist, and although it took years and at times seemed extremely unlikely, it came to pass because I continued to strive toward this goal. Now that I am a psychologist, I rarely think about my missteps or all the errors I made. Yes, it hurt to experience them, and it felt horrible to fail, but now I realize those hardships taught me the true value of patience, consistency, loyalty, and other great skills I never thought I needed. In the end, my work paid off and God kept his promise. But my doctoral degree was never the ultimate goal. It was just the beginning of a commitment God made to me, and I needed to go through the process of making some significant life adjustments before I accomplished my dream. God wanted to give me a spiritual diploma in areas only he could teach and acquiring a degree in psychology was just part of the plan.

Graduate school was just one part of a larger spiritual journey I had to live through. God used it to help me figure out my purpose before I received his promises. Needless to say, it taught me *a lot*. I learned what my strengths and weaknesses were. School also forced me to step outside of my comfort zone so I could be a little more independent. In addition to this, I became skilled at ignoring distractions. I also mastered the art of letting certain people go. Most importantly, I finally understood how much God wanted to establish a loving relationship with me. In fact, in the midst of all my crises, God would gently speak, and then encourage me to keep believing in him by reminding me of his wonderful promises. The Bible, says, "For no matter how many promises God has made, they are 'Yes' in Christ. And so, through him the 'Amen' is spoken by us to the glory of God" (2 Corinthians 1:20; NIV). The 'yes' in Christ means, God keeps his commitments. He is consistent, loyal, and cannot renege on what he said. But in order to receive his promises, I had to agree with what God said he would do. The 'amen' had to come from me.

Dr. Brandy S. Peoples
10 hrs

"You have to agree with God's promises if you want to receive them."

God used the challenges I faced to help me pinpoint the spiritual issues that kept me from saying 'amen' to his promises. I didn't fully trust God, and from time to time, I devised a backup plan just in case his promises fell through. The Biblical story of Abraham and Sarah is a great example of this. They were a couple who faced a very intimate trial, and although they were given a promise, they let doubt get in the way of their agreement with what God planned for them (see Genesis chapters 15-21). Here's their story. Abraham and Sarah had amassed great wealth, and if this were modern times, they probably would have owned tailor made clothes, luxury cars, vacation homes, and private jets. But out of all the things they possessed, Abraham asked, "Sovereign Lord, what can you give me since I remain childless... (Genesis 15:2; NIV). Sarah was barren and had given up on her dream of being a mother. But one day, God promised the couple a child. In fact, he promised Abraham so many descendants that he wouldn't be able to count them. This seemed rather far-fetched. Abraham believed, but Sarah didn't trust what she was hearing.

Reasonably speaking, Sarah was hurt, and this made it hard for her to agree with God's promise. She decided to take matters into her own hands. Sarah came up with a more practical way of having a child. Sarah talked Abraham into sleeping with her maid, Hagar, so she could be a stepmother! Unfortunately, the consequences of this huge faux pas did not manifest until well after Abraham's son, Ishmael was born. But then, out of the blue, God said, "...your wife Sarah will bear you a son, and you will call him Isaac" (Genesis 17:19; NIV). God confirmed his promise again through three angels. But Sarah's response was to skeptically laugh. I don't blame her though. Not having a child probably caused her so much pain that the only thing she could do was laugh to keep from crying. To her surprise, after years of tests and trials, "Sarah became preg-

87

nant and bore a son to Abraham in his old age, at the very time God had promised him. Abraham gave the name Isaac to the son Sarah bore him" (Genesis 21:2-3; NIV). God's promise prevailed.

Oftentimes, the issues that we haven't dealt with can prevent us from agreeing with God's promises. For instance, even though God promised the couple a son, they didn't completely trust him, and as a result, Sarah convinced Abraham to sleep with another woman. Some might say Sarah was mostly to blame, but let's not forget, Abraham also agreed with this arrangement. So it's likely they both wrestled with doubt. Because of their joint issues, Abraham and Sarah thought it was best to rely on their own plan instead of a guaranteed promise from God. In the end, neither of them considered the severity of their mistake until Sarah began to take issue with Ishmael's mother, Hagar, and she asked Abraham to send them away. He reluctantly agreed. But it was too late, Abraham and Sarah let their painful issues shape their choices instead of focusing on God's promise which would determine their next plan of action.

 **Dr. Brandy S. Peoples**
10 hrs ·

"Trust God's promises and not your own plans."

God's promise was inevitable, and it was sure to come to pass. When he first spoke to Abraham, God promised him, "I will make you into a great nation, and I will bless you" (Genesis 12:1; NIV). Ultimately, God wanted to use Isaac to give birth to a nation called the Israelites. But at the time, Abraham did not realize God wanted to bless him with *many* descendants, and not just one. Years later, God also made a promise to the Israelites that was similar to what he made to their forefather, Abraham. God told them, "Take possession of the land and settle in it, for I have given you the land to possess" (Numbers 33:53; NIV). At first, this promise sounds contradictory. How could the Israelites possess something they had already been given? But like I said earlier, God has a very distinct way of doing things. To better understand this paradoxical promise, let's back up a bit.

First off, God exists outside of time, and he has proclaimed the end, at the beginning. This means God knows the future, and he knew all about the Israelites, well before they were even a nation. Therefore, God knew their future circumstances and why they would need to possess land (see Exodus chapter 1). The Israelites were an oppressed group of people who had been enslaved by the Egyptian Pharaoh for hundreds of years. When they were finally freed by Moses, they had nothing to show for their labor, so they needed land. With it, they could safely settle, build homes, raise animals, farm crops, and start families. More families meant more children, and more children meant more descendants for Abraham. God wanted to fulfill the promise that he had made to him, and he was using the Israelites to do it.

Dr. Brandy S. Peoples
10 hrs ·

"God makes promises because he wants to do something through you, for generations to come, and not just for you in the present time."

God promised Abraham, "The whole land of Canaan, where you reside as a foreigner, I will *give as an everlasting possession to you and your descendants after you*; and I will be their God"(Genesis 17:8; NIV emphasis mine). From the very beginning, God wanted to bless Abraham and all of his descendants with the land of Canaan, now, let's explore the deeper meaning of some of these words in context. If I were to summarize, God told the Israelites, "Take *possession* of land that I have already *given* you." The word *give* is pretty much self-explanatory, and it is based on God's time which is future-oriented. The word *possess* means to *control, occupy,* or *own*. When you possess something, you own it. Therefore, it is believed that well before the Israelites were enslaved, and then released, God had already *given* them land to *control, occupy,* and *own*.

Although God had already given them land, possessing it would be a bit more complicated. In order to possess the land, the Israelites had to agree with God's Word. But once they reached and surveyed the Promised Land, some of them returned with a bad report, and said, "The land we explored devours those living in it. All the people we saw there are of great size" (Numbers 13:32; NIV). Yes, the Canaanites, who were already living there, were bigger and appeared like giants to the Israelites, but with God, they could have easily defeated them. In spite of this, many of the Israelites let pessimism get the best of them. Others were afraid. Then there were those who grumbled and complained about God. Some even suggested going back to Egypt! The Israelites were physically free but psychologically enslaved.

Dr. Brandy S. Peoples
10 hrs · 🌐

"Your mindset can prevent you from getting what God has promised you."

The Canaanites were not the only giants the Israelites had to fight. They had another more personal battle to win. The Israelites needed to reclaim their mind and kill the giant called negative thinking. Their negative mindset kept them from agreeing with God's promise and immediately possessing the land. But this was not a surprise to God. He knew what their issues were. I believe he parted the Red Sea because he wanted them to see that they had the all-powerful God on their side. This should have built their confidence. But once they saw the Canaanites, they became afraid. The Israelites could not get past their fear, and it would take them an additional 40 years of wandering in the desert before they changed their crippled mindset, which God tested and renewed. In the end, a new generation of Israelites led by Joshua and Caleb (two of the original surveyors of the land) were mentally prepared to possess the promise. They made it to the Promised Land.

Please do not think that God only makes promises about descendants or acquiring land. Also, I definitely don't want you to think that it will take 40 years before you get what God has promised you. All of these things are simply used as metaphors. The "land" in your life could be anything God has promised you. It could be a house, marriage, or even a successful business. But whatever the "land" is, remember God says, "For I have given you the land to possess" (Numbers 33:53; NIV). So tell yourself, "God has given me good health," "God has given me a great job," "God has given me a successful marriage." God has given all of his children amazing gifts. If you receive it, is solely dependent on your willingness to fully agree with the promise. Therefore, possessing them is up to you. So, pursue your purpose. Take control of your life. Own the talents you've been given. Occupy this earthly kingdom which is only one phase of Jesus Christ's rule. He has already given us a heavenly kingdom. It is up to us if we want to possess it.

Things to Consider:

What is your promised land? Is it improved health, a new job, a brand-new home? Whatever it is, substitute it in this sentence, "I have given you _____ for you to possess."

What keeps you from possessing it? How can you defeat the "giants" that are currently occupying your territory?

Write down all of God's promises to you. Whenever you start to doubt what he has said, read them for encouragement.

What are your special abilities, talents, and gifts? How can you use them to possess what God has promised you?

Given that Jesus promises us residence in an eternal kingdom, which kingdom are you prepared to possess? Your actions will determine your citizenship.

Conclusion

By now, you should know that we all have a purpose. In fact, every created being on the planet has been purposed to live for God in a way that best fits their divine design. There are those who are exceptionally wise versus others who have an uncanny knack to lead in times of distress. Some of us are amazingly creative while others are extremely faithful. In my case, God blessed me with wisdom, knowledge, teaching, counseling, and speaking abilities. He then took me through an arduous process where he developed those skills and more. During that time, I learned incredibly useful things needed for my profession. But God also taught me unbelievable spiritual skills that are essential to my life. Now, I'm a psychologist and a minister. My purpose is to glorify God using these blessings.

Whatever it is you have been given, God intends for you to use it to glorify him. So ask yourself, what can you do? The process of figuring this out may not be easy. The people you meet. Obstacles you face. Your successes. Your failures. All of these things can be used to help you to find your purpose. Sometimes you'll have to step outside of your comfort zone and wait to hear from God for it. Though you may wander and feel confused. Do not give up. You are a royal character in God's story and everything you need has been strategically put in place to prepare you for kingdom living on Earth and in heaven. Trust in his plan, and you will see that God loves you. In fact, God's love is personified in Jesus Christ and the Holy Spirit. All three of them are needed if you want to access the authority and power you've been given to push through the dirty circumstances of life. Freely accept their help, because what you do on Earth will determine your future spiritual citizenship. Ultimately, the journey toward purpose will never cease, it will continue into eternity, which is the ultimate promise.

About the Author

Dr. Brandy S. Peoples is from St. Louis, Missouri. She is a licensed psychologist and an ordained minister. Dr. Peoples works in the areas of forensic and clinical psychology. She is actively involved with her church and serves on the administrative and ministerial teams. In her spare time, she loves to work out and is a self-proclaimed "fashionista." On a typical weekend she binge watches sci-fi/fantasy television shows. Out of all of her accomplishments, Dr. Peoples is most proud of being a servant-leader who is committed to teaching about mental health awareness and preaching the Gospel of the Kingdom of God.

For booking inquiries contact:
dr.brandy@drbrandyspeoples.com
or at www.drbrandyspeoples.com

Made in the USA
Columbia, SC
26 April 2021